Constant, YET Ever-Changing

A HISTORIC OVERVIEW *of* CONTINUED REVELATION

Constant, YET Ever-Changing

A HISTORIC OVERVIEW of CONTINUED REVELATION

DANIEL BARKER

CFI
An imprint of Cedar Fort, Inc.
Springville, Utah

ISBN 13: 978-1-4621-3890-6

Published by CFI, an imprint of Cedar Fort, Inc.
2373 W. 700 S., Springville, UT, 84663
Distributed by Cedar Fort, Inc., www.cedarfort.com

Library of Congress Control Number: 2021931733

Cover design by Shawnda T. Craig

Printed in the United States of America

10 9 8 7 6 5 4 3 2 1

Printed on acid-free paper

Contents

Preface

Change is constant. In The Church of Jesus Christ of Latter-day Saints there is no side-stepping change. It's the way the world rolls these days. Chad M. Orton and William W. Slaughter, in their book *Joseph Smith's America,* stated, "One modern think tank has estimated that prior to the birth of Jesus Christ, new ideas, including scientific inventions and improved ways of doing things, were produced annually at the rate of 39 a year. During Joseph Smith's lifetime, that number exploded to 3, 840 a year—a nearly 1,000% increase. Today an estimated 110,000 changes occur each year—a 280% increase over the nineteenth century."[1]

Some changes are natural and painless to implement, while others are more difficult to embrace. We don't always have to accept change. We can fight if we so choose. However, in some cases, we don't always have the freedom of choice. For instance, in the mid-1970s, during my high school years, Canada was in the process of adopting change whether we wanted it or not. The Canadian government at the time opted to switch from the imperial system of measuring to the metric system. Similar to the citizens of the United States, Canadians were accustomed to speaking in terms of measuring in inches, feet, yards, miles, pounds, miles per hour, Fahrenheit, and acres. My world was quickly turned upside down when I was now required to answer math questions in millimeters, centimeters, and meters. I now weighed myself in kilograms (the fastest weight lost program out there). On the road, I was now required to convert from miles and miles per hour, something I understood and was comfortable with, into something completely foreign to me, kilometers and kilometers per hour. Land measurements would now be spoken of in terms of hectares (what?). At the gas station I no longer purchased gas in gallons but in liters. And finally, how hot or cold is twenty degrees Celsius? A few years prior to the change, radio spots aired educating the public in preparation for the go-live date. I think my friends and I looked at this as a necessary evil and so, while complaining, slowly embraced the new system. A few gas stations rebelled at the imposed change and continued selling in gallons. This attitude led to a head-on collision with the authorities, which dealt the corresponding retribution. It was interesting viewing speed limit signs, stating 110. For a flicker of a moment I thought it was time to put the pedal to the metal but realized after a fast calculation that this was actually 65 miles per hour.

The Church is no different. The history of The Church of Jesus Christ of Latter-day Saints is replete with examples from a plethora of change. Similar to Canada, and the renovation of the old system of measuring, some transformations in the Church came hard. Polygamy comes to mind, both at its inception and cessation of the practice. On the flip side, other change in the Church was viewed by many optimistically, with compliance to the change easy and automatic. A two-hour meeting block, the switch to nineteen-year-old sister missionaries, and the option of eighteen-year-old elders was positively regarded by the Saints. An encouraging alteration from my youth was bishops were no longer required to plead for money from the pulpit to replenish a draining ward budget; Church funds would now come to the rescue. Other change arrived with mixed reviews, such as members now acting as weekend warriors, also known as Saturday-morning janitors.

In midst of the number of revisions over time, there will be those who embrace it and those who find it hard to acclimate. For instance, as mentioned above, as exciting as it was for young people permitted full-time missionary status at a younger age, there were some that didn't experience the same enthusiasm. This is part of the mystery of change. Because we are individuals, what might be new and exciting to one may be viewed by another as a turn in the wrong direction.

But this isn't what this book is about—the common, more talked and taught about changes, that is. To be honest, there's enough revision during the course of history in the Church to fill volumes. If this isn't enough, much has been written on the history of these modifications. Why should I write something you already know? Because there's not much interest in that. This book looks at the more unique changes to practices in the Church. So, when I previously indicated there has been a plethora of change, what I actually meant is plethora to the max (I share sixty-six unique changes in the coming pages). For instance, did you know at one time (1920s) that Primary children, eight to twelve years of age, could attend the temple and do baptisms for the dead? Did you also realize, prior to the Saints leaving Nauvoo, that very young individuals were married for time and eternity? You ask how young (after all, I was twenty-two, my wife was twenty when we were sealed, and that's young, but not unusual). How does twelve years old sound to you? Also, the sacrament in the early Utah Church was not performed the way we take the sacrament today. During the pioneer years, talks were given and hymns sung while the sacrament was administered and passed to those who were either standing, sitting, or kneeling. In addition, the wine goblet and tray of bread were passed from person to person, row by row, together. Believe it or not, the Saints established a new alphabet, having gone so far as to print portions of the Book of Mormon using the characters from the new writing system. We have numerous choices of missions today—I'm sure a wider array than the early Church—but to be honest, the mission calls during early Utah Territory were definitely exceptionally unique. For instance, what in the world was the Rag Mission?

The above examples serve as teasers with the hope that you will dive into the following pages. As you read this book you will discover that change in the early Church was alive and well, the way it is today, and that we have always evolved. Some of the practices I bring to light were Church-wide, while others were the result of the discretion of a particular bishop or stake president. Regardless, whether at the ward level, or globally, it was a practice that no longer exists today.

In a sense, we do the same thing today. The Church has standardized the way the sacrament is presently passed. However, the sacrament isn't so structured that there isn't room for differences from ward to ward. Think about it. How many different configurations, or the way the deacons line up during the passing of the sacrament, have you seen?

I think most members can count maybe half a dozen various ways that can vary from congregation to congregation.

Where I'm able to determine why the practice was done away, I will share this too since the cessation of the rituals are just as interesting as the change itself.

At the conclusion of this book you might be of the same belief as I am that our daily routines are very different from that of the pioneer Saints. However, when it comes to the Church and change, we are like peas in a pod. There isn't a Saint out there today who doesn't sit down to view general conference and wonder what the prophet will announce that will be the hot topic of conversations the next day. The same was true of the pioneer Church. There wasn't a family who entered the Tabernacle for general conference during the 1800s who didn't wonder if the father, or the entire family, would be called over the pulpit to serve a mission to a far-off corner of the world, or to strengthen an established ward, or pioneer a new colony along the "Mormon Corridor."

The scope of this book is not to be a detailed study of the changes mentioned, but rather an introduction of what we used to do in the Church, compared to what we do now. This book is meant to be an easy-to-read, fun look at change in the Church and not written to provide additional scholarly knowledge to the seasoned historian. I found information for a number of subjects that I touched on in academic articles, journals, and books. For those wishing to research further, additional academic information can be found in the following:

- *The Joseph Smith Papers*
- *BYU Studies*
- *Gospel Topics Essay* (ChurchofJesusChrist.org)
- *The Journal of Mormon History*
- *Mormon Historical Studies*
- *Revelations in Context* (churchofjesuschrist.org/study/manual/revelations-in-context)
- *Journal History*
- Foundation for Ancient Research and Mormon Studies (FARMS)

On occasion I suggest other sources, over and beyond what I used, which provides further insight into the topic.

To some, these changes may be disconcerting. However, when you realize we believe in modern revelation, it shouldn't be surprising that the Church has evolved and will continue to do so. As great as this is, what's more satisfying is knowing that we will continue to be part of historic change in the Church. It was exciting for me to read various early members' journals and autobiography accounts who experienced these changes, and to discover what life was like for those who lived in Kirtland, Missouri, Nauvoo, and Utah Territory. You, too, will find excitement as you record the changes we are experiencing currently. You will excite future generations as they read your journal of the modifications you experienced, your role in the change, and your thoughts and feelings on the alterations. Because of the Church's history, what is taking place today, and understanding that this will continue into the future, we are led to say, "We thank thee, O God, for a prophet" and are ever so grateful for a loving Father in Heaven who knows us and exemplifies this love through continued revelation.

Administering to the Sick

Similar to biblical times, men with authority in this dispensation have blessed the sick and oppressed. This is one of the signs of those who profess to belong to the Church of Christ. In the early years of the Church, there were those whose search for the gospel culminated at the waters of baptism, due in large part from witnessing a healing. Ezra Booth was one such individual. He was a Methodist minister during the Kirtland years of the Church and by circumstance happened to be in the room when Joseph Smith healed the afflicted arm of Elsa Johnson.[1] Here's another example. Joseph Smith was traveling home to Kirtland from a conference held in Orange, Ohio, with William E. McLellin when the following incident occurred. William records the scene:

> I stepped off of a large log and strained my ankle very badly—thence I rode; and just as I was abo[u]t to start to bed I asked brother Joseph what he thought about my ancle's being healed. He immediately turned to me and asked me if I believed in my heart that God through his instrumentality would heal it. I answered that I believed he would. He laid his hands on it and it was healed although It was swelled much and had pained me severely.[2]

In the Kirtland Temple in 1836 Joseph Smith introduced the use of consecrated oil in the healing ritual to the Saints.[3] We continue this today. I've had the privilege of anointing and blessing family members and friends. It was a special opportunity when I visited a friend in the hospital and prior to leaving provided a blessing. It didn't seem odd when the individual who occupied the same room with my colleague requested a blessing. Residing in Utah at the time of this incident, I assumed the individual asking for a blessing was a member of the Church. Through conversation it became apparent he was a member of another faith. I've experienced this before, mind you many years ago while serving as a missionary. It gave me an opportunity to explain to this individual the sacred nature of blessings and why we perform them in the Church. Feeling confident he understood the principle of this ordinance that he was soliciting, the anticipated blessing was provided. As trained, my partner placed consecrated oil on this man's head.

This is the way we do it today, anointing the crown of the head with oil. However, it might amaze you that this isn't the way the anointing with oil was always performed through the history of the Church.

A favorite pioneer of mine is Mosiah Hancock. Mosiah records the following in his autobiography:

> When we got to Cash Cave we met father and Brother David Pettigrew going back to the bluff for us [most likely Council Bluff]. So father returned with us to the valley. While we were going down East Canyon Creek mother's foot got caught in between the box and wagon tongue and broke the toe at the upper joint; but the skin was not broken. So father anointed her foot there and administered to her and it was healed quite soon.[4]

Similar to the Joseph Smith/William E. McLellin account, Levi also administered oil to the injured body part, which indicates this practice was common for those asking for and receiving a blessing. Never in my years in the Church did anyone tell me this was typical of early anointings. I only assumed that since we placed consecrated oil on the crown of the head that this is the way it has always remained from the days of Jesus Christ and Joseph Smith. When I came across a third instance of this procedure, it confirmed to me that this was indeed a common practice in the early days of the Church and a practice that followed the Saints to Utah.

Many pioneers understood Ephraim Hanks was richly blessed with the gift of healing—not just for the members of the Church but also for native tribes from Missouri to the Salt Lake Valley. Those tribes that understood Ephraim considered him an individual who communicated with the "Great Spirit." During the winter of 1857, while Brother Hanks was hauling mail from Salt Lake City to Independence, Missouri, he was touched by the Spirit to visit a Sioux tribe in the area. When he entered the village, a boy was carried to him on a buffalo robe. The boy was unable to move and had failed to moved for a number of months after being thrown from his horse. Ephraim asked for the boys' clothing to be removed, after which "Elder Hanks anointed the afflicted parts with consecrated oil, which he always carried with him, and then administered to him in the name of Jesus Christ, promising that he should be made whole from that very moment. The boy immediately arose from his bed of affliction and walked out of the lodge, to the astonishment of all who saw."[5]

We're familiar with the current day practice of anointing the crown of the head with consecrated oil, and now we understand the pioneer practice of directly anointing injured body parts. Nevertheless, as amazing as it may seem, there was a third application for the oil. One of the websites I thoroughly enjoyed reading in the past is the Book of Abraham Project (www.boap.org). As part of this project, numerous autobiographies and journals were collected from various contemporaries of the Prophet Joseph Smith and placed in one easy-to-find location. Through this website I discovered Mosiah Hancock and immersed myself in his autobiography. Another autobiography found in this project is that of Benjamin Brown. Through Brother Brown I discovered the third method of applying consecrated oil and how he anointed an individual when called on to administer to a sick sister during the Nauvoo period of the Church: "The oil arriving, we administered some to her internally, in the name of the Lord, when she arouse without assistance."[6]

Sarah Pea Rich, while residing at Garden Grove, Iowa, describes the process of nursing George Patten, a young man living with the Rich family, from an illness. The ritual included both the rubbing of consecrated oil on his face and head and consuming internally the oil, a teaspoon at a time.[7]

The previously mentioned situations are not obscure incidents. In fact, there's enough evidence to suggest the anointing of injured body parts and the internal consumption of consecrated oil were common from the inception of the latter-day Church and continued until the twentieth century.

So, why don't we practice this today? In the 1950s Church leaders openly taught that administering to the sick and anointing with consecrated oil was to be on the head only. Judging from Elder Joseph Fielding Smith's statement, it appears there was nothing theologically wrong with ingesting consecrated oil, other than the conviction of some Church members at the time of increased healing powers if consumed. The ordinance of healing the sick is largely dependent on the faith of the individual receiving the anointing and administration and therefore is not conditional on the placement of oil on injured body parts. The bottom line is, we do what our leaders ask us to do, and due to the potential for "impropriety" of the placement of consecrated oil on body parts we refrain and anoint on the crown of the head only. The following from Joseph Fielding Smith:

> "Is it proper to anoint the afflicted parts of the body?"
>
> No. The anointing should be on the crown of the head. (It could be a matter of impropriety to anoint afflicted parts of the body.)
>
> "Is it permissible to administer the oil internally?"
>
> No. Taking the oil internally is not part of the administration. If persons who are ill wish to take oil internally, they are not forbidden, but many sicknesses will not be improved by oil in the stomach.[8]

Finally, Elder Bruce R. McConkie shares the following: "Taking consecrated oil internally, or using it for anointing or rubbing afflicted parts of the body, is not part of the ordinance of administering to the sick."[9]

NOTES

1. *Early Scenes in Church History: Four Faith Promoting Classics, Philo Dibble Autobiography* (Salt Lake City: Bookcraft, 1968), 74–96.
2. *The Journals of William E. McLellin, 1831–1836*, ed. Jan Shipps and John W. Welch (Provo, UT: BYU Studies; Urbana and Chicago: University of Illinois Press, 1994), 45.
3. rsc/byu.edu/our-rites-worship/pouring-oil-development-modern-mormon-healing-ritual.
4. *Autobiography of Mosiah Hancock*, Typescript, BYU-S; boap.org
5. Stewart E. Glazier and Robert S. Clark, *Journey of the Trail* (Salt Lake City: The Church of Jesus Christ of Latter-day Saints, 1997), 120–21.
6. Autobiography of Benjamin Brown; boap.org
7. Ivan J. Barrett, *Heroic Mormon Women* (Covenant Communications, Inc.: American Fork, Utah, 2000), 27–28.
8. Joseph Fielding Smith, *Answers to Gospel Questions* (Salt Lake City: Deseret Book Co., 1957), 1:148.
9. Bruce R. McConkie, *Mormon Doctrine* (Salt Lake City: Bookcraft, 1966), 22.

Administrations to the Sick (Women)

The following is shared in in the Gospel Topic essays on churchofjesuschrist.org:

> Joseph Smith organized the Relief Society as part of the structure of the Church, which formally defined and authorized a major aspect of women's ministry. All this was done to prepare the Saints to participate in the ordinances of the temple, which were introduced soon after the founding of the Relief Society. At the time of his death, the revelatory vision imparted to Joseph Smith was securely in place: women and men could receive and administer sacred priesthood ordinances in holy temples, which would help prepare them to enter the presence of God one day.[1]

The following are examples from Church history that point to the fact that women participated in the administration of the sick. From the journal of Julina Lambson Smith, February 14, 1886, we read: "Sister Coles came to be administered to. She has a large lump growing in her Opu [stomach or womb]. It pains her considerably. Sister Young anointed the affected part, and Jos. Albert with some of the other Elders administered to her."[2]

This entry is from the journal of Patty Bartlett Sessions: "March 17, 1847. . . . Mr. Sessions and I went and laid hands on the widow Holmans step daughter. She was healed."[3]

And finally, Mary Isabella Horne wrote about her daughter's healing: "[She] was taken very ill, and her life despaired of, in fact it seemed impossible for her to get better. The mother of the Prophet, Mrs. Lucy Smith, came and blessed the child, and said she should live. This was something new in that age, for a woman to administer to the sick."[4]

From assisting, to anointing with consecrated oil, to serving as the mouth during an administration, women in the early history of The Church of Jesus Christ of Latter-day Saints were active participants in the healing of the sick. As early as the Nauvoo years, Joseph Smith, and continuing to John Taylor, the first three prophets of the Church shared their sentiments pertaining to women taking part in the blessing and healing of the sick. On April 28, 1842, a little more than a month after the organization of the Relief Society (March 17, 1842), Joseph Smith stated: "Respecting females administering for the healing of the sick . . . there could be no evil in it, if God gave His sanction by healing; that there could be no more sin in any female laying hands on and praying for the sick, than in wetting the face with water; it is no sin for anybody to administer that has faith, or if the sick have faith to be healed by their administrations."[5]

I have a faint memory of waking in the morning and having one eye sealed partially closed by sleep. Because I was a little guy and not understanding why I couldn't open my eye, of course I was panicked and ran down the hallway from my bedroom to the kitchen, calling out to my mother. In her loving, soothing way, she scooped me into her arms, took me into the bathroom, and with a warm, moist cloth gently washed my eyelashes. It wasn't the fear of losing sight in one eye so much that I remember from this situation, but more so the gentle touch of a member of the Relief Society. This was Joseph Smith's justification. It was the loving, soothing, caring touch of the women of the Church. Joseph Smith shared the following:

> Who are better qualified to administer than our faithful and zealous sisters, whose hearts are full of faith, tenderness, sympathy, and compassion? No one. I gave a lecture on the priesthood, showing how the sisters could come in possession of the privileges, blessings, and gifts of the priesthood, and that the signs should follow them, such as healing the sick, casting out devils, etc. And that they might attain unto these blessings by virtuous life and conversation, and diligence in keeping all the commandments.[6]

Brigham Young taught at a Nauvoo General Conference in 1844, "I want a Wife that can take care of my chi[ldre]n when I am away—who can pray—lay on hands anoint with oil and baffle the enemy."[7]

Then again in 1869, Brigham Young, directing his comments to the mothers in Zion, said: "Why do you not live so as to rebuke disease? It is your privilege to do so without sending for the Elders. . . . It is the privilege of a mother to have faith and to administer to her child; this she can do herself, as well as sending for the Elders to have the benefit of their faith."[8]

The propriety and the right bestowed on the Relief Society to perform this ordinance was never a question with the early prophets in this dispensation. A number of years ago, a newly converted couple joined my ward. Being new in the gospel, they were enthusiastic and soaking it all in. They read as much as they could and participated in the ward both socially and through callings, developing into strong advocates for genealogy and the temple. I remember the day when one of my children was sick. I contacted this brother and asked if he would assist me in giving my child a blessing. It wasn't long before he appeared on our front doorstep with his wife. We visited and then commenced to perform the anointing. Just as we were preparing to anoint, this dear sister commented that women used to participate in blessings and felt that all the help in our home at the time, both priesthood and Relief Society, could muster the faith to have our child healed. I had never heard of this before. How could this be? They were new to the Church. I was a lifelong member, a seminary graduate, a returned missionary, and the current elders quorum president of my ward. Never once had I recalled being taught that women administered to the sick. I wasn't quite sure what she was suggesting and was relieved when she stopped short of placing her hands on my child's head, but rather stood beside her husband with bowed head and folded arms.

John Taylor clarified the rights that the Relief Society held regarding administrations when he taught the following in the fall of 1880:

> It is the privilege of all faithful women and lay members of the Church, who believe in Christ, to administer to all the sick or afflicted in their respective families, either by the laying on of hands, or by the anointing with oil in the name of the Lord: but they should administer in these sacred ordinances, not by virtue and authority of the priesthood, but by virtue of their faith in Christ, and the promises made to believers: and thus they should do in all their ministrations.[9]

Armed with permission from God's spokesman on earth, the sisters didn't disappoint. However, judging by what I've read through the years, the Relief Society didn't abuse this power, either. In fact, it appears that women administered to the sick, generally in the absence of the priesthood. To be honest, how often did a mother find herself alone during the early years of the Church? Trust me, it happened more than we care to admit. There were missions, Zion's Camp, death at the hands of mobs in both Missouri and Illinois, the Mormon Battalion, and the first vanguard company of the Saints to the Salt Lake Valley. It was essential for women to be bestowed with this right simply because a priesthood holder was not always present in the home.[10] As an example, Betsy Jane Simons, a widow and resident of Quincy, Illinois, at the time, experienced frustration by the fact that a priesthood holder simply could not be found in her surrounding area. Faced with this dilemma, she records:

> All at once as distinct as though someone had spoken to me [a voice said], "Why don't you administer to him yourself?" I was anxious for my lady friend to depart that I might administer as the spirit directed. In a few moments she left. . . . Alone I could unburden my heart and pour out my soul in earnest prayer to my Father in heaven. Kneeling by the bed on which lay my dying child, it should be an evidence to me that it was my duty to sell my home and come to the valley. . . . I administered to him and he was healed.[11]

Louisa B. Pratt's husband, Addison, served numerous missions for the Church and was absent for extended periods of time. He was gone for almost five years to the Society Islands (1844–48).[12] Sister Pratt tells of her young daughter, who, during the Saints' sojourn in Nauvoo, was exposed to smallpox, which, shortly after this contact, developed into a fever. Worried for her daughter's health, Louisa reached out to the priesthood to provide the healing administration. Try as she might, Louisa failed to succeed in convincing the "frightened elders" to administer to her sick daughter. Louisa Pratt records what happened next: "The devil shall not have power thus to afflict me. I then laid hands on my child and rebuked the fever. . . . In a few days the fever was gone."[13]

In conjunction with blessings of healings, women also provided blessings of comfort to each other. Many incidents have been revealed in the journals of women blessing women. Again, Patty Bartlett Sessions provides us with one such occasion:

> Fair weather. We expect to start tomorrow for the mountains. I called to Sarah Anns this evening with E. R. Snow. Sisters Whitney and Kimball came in. We had a good time. Things were

> given to us that we were not to tell of but to ponder them in our hearts and profit thereby. Before we went down there E. Beaman, Eliza or Emily Partridge, Zina Jacobs came here laid their hands on my head blessed me and so did E. R. Snow. Thank the Lord.[14]

It wasn't until the 1920s when the practice of women giving blessings of healing and comfort began to fade. In the recent Gospel Topics essays published by the Church, we learn, "Women's participation in healing blessings gradually declined in the early 20th century as Church leaders taught that it was preferable to follow the New Testament directive to 'call for the elders.' By 1926, Church President Heber J. Grant affirmed that the First Presidency 'do not encourage calling in the sisters to administer to the sick, as the scriptures tell us to call in the Elders, who hold the priesthood of God and have the power and authority to administer to the sick in the name of Jesus Christ.'"[15]

After 1946, the practice ceased entirely when Elder Joseph Fielding Smith issued the following statement in a letter to the Relief Societies of the church: "While the authorities of the Church have ruled that it is permissible, under certain conditions and with the approval of the priesthood, for sisters to wash and anoint other sisters, yet they feel that it is far better to follow the plan the Lord has given us and send for the Elders of the Church to come and minister to the sick and afflicted."[16]

Currently, the Church Handbook explains, "Only worthy Melchizedek Priesthood holders may administer to the sick or afflicted."[17]

NOTES

1. churchofjesuschrist.org/study/manual/gospel-topics-essays/joseph-smiths-teachings-about-priesthood-temple-women?lang=eng
2. Kenneth W. Godfrey, Audrey M. Godfrey, and Jill Mulvay Derr, *Women's Voices: An Untold History of The Latter-day Saints 1830–1900* (Salt Lake City: Deseret Book Company, 1982), 354.
3. *The Diaries of Perrigrine Sessions,* comp. Earl T. Sessions (Bountiful, Utah: Carr Printing Co., 1967).
4. Anonymous, "A Representative Woman: Mary Isabella Horne," *Woman's Exponent* 11 (June 15, 1882), 9.
5. Discourse, 28 April 1842, as reported by Eliza R. Snow, page 36 as found in the josephsmithpapers.org; *History of the Church,* volume 4, 604.

6. Ivan J. Barrett, *Heroic Mormon Women* (Covenant Communications, Inc.: American Fork, Utah, 2000), 27–28.
7. Thomas Bullock account of Brigham Young sermon, Special Elders Meeting, April 9, 1844, in Church Historian's Office, General Church Minutes, 1839–1877, *Selected Collections,* 1:18.
8. Brigham Young, Sermon, November 14, 1869, *Journal of Discourses,* 13:155.
9. Quorum of the Twelve Apostles, Circular Letter, October 6, 1880, microfilm of holograph, CR 2 30.
10. Plewe, Brandon S., et. at., *Mapping Mormonism* (Provo, Utah: Brigham Young University Press, 2012), 42.
11. Claudia Bushman, *Mormon Sisters: Women in Early Utah* (BYU Studies: Provo, Utah, 1997), 23.
12. Plewe, Brandon S., et al., *Mapping Mormonism* (Provo, Utah: Brigham Young University Press, 2012), 42.
13. Vicky Burgess-Olsen, *Sister Saints* (Vicky Burgess-Olsen: 1978), 50–51.
14. *The Diaries of Perrigrine Sessions,* comp. Earl T. Sessions (Bountiful, Utah: Carr Printing Co., 1967).
15. "Joseph Smith's Teachings about Priesthood, Temple, and Women," Gospel Topics Essay, ChurchofJesusChrist.org.
16. Ibid.
17. *General Handbook: Serving in The Church of Jesus Christ of Latter-day Saints,* 18.13.1.

For additional information see "Joseph Smith's Teachings about Priesthood, Temple, and Women," Gospel Topics Essay, ChurchofJesusChrist.org.

Adoption, The Law of

William Clayton reports the following excerpt from a discourse given by Joseph Smith in April 1844:

> As a last extremity like a nail in a sure place—he says "else what shall they do who are bap for the dead &c" We have come to the last dispensation & must have all the [that] God has to give—all the baptism. H. G. [Holy Ghost] &c—If the dead rise not why are you baptised for them if they are to lay in the grave forever—plan devised

> around the eternal throne of God—established by Paul. brought to light by Joseph—and the man that will lift his voice against it is a heard harted retch unfit to preach the gospel. has a figure—the Habeas Corpus the L. D. S [Latter Day Saints] know what H. C [Habeas Corpus] means—have reason—have laid down an eternal fiat law of adoption into the k of G. [kingdom of God] I have shewed that many good have died without this privilege.[1]

The law of adoption was practiced in The Church of Jesus Christ of Latter-day Saints from 1846 to 1894. Some may not be familiar with this doctrine now, but at the time of its popularity, during the little time remaining in Nauvoo, spilling over into Winter Quarters, and finally, somewhat in the Salt Lake Valley, many men and women were adopted to leading authorities in the Church. If the pioneer Saints had the understanding of temple ordinances and work for the dead that it did commencing with Wilford Woodruff and the St. George temple in 1877, this principle may never have existed. However, as mentioned in the preface of this book, the Church has always evolved as additional revelation is provided, particularly the doctrines taught in relation to the temple. Changes have been made, leading to the extinction or modification of previous practices, such as the law of adoption. Brigham Young stated, "Joseph in his life time did not receive every thing connected with the doctrine of redemption, but he has left the key with those who understand how to obtain and teach to this great people all that is necessary for their salvation and exaltation in the celestial kingdom of our God."[2]

The reasoning behind it begins with Joseph Smith and his understanding of a welding link from father to son.[3] Carl J. Cranney states:

> Under Brigham's leadership, Saints begin sealing couples to priesthood leaders—called adoption. . . . The reason for sealing couples to priesthood leaders was ostensibly to connect families to the priesthood. Because many of the Saints did not have extended family in the church (almost everybody was a first-generation convert), they needed to be sealed to those who had the 'right' of the priesthood, based on their then-current understanding of Doctrine and Covenants 86:8–10, which speaks of 'lawful heirs' whose priesthood comes from their "lineage" and which priesthood "must needs remain through you and your lineage.[4]

The concern was real for many of the first generation converts and the understanding that "they would be left without priesthood connection to the family of God."[5] These adoptions were solidified in the Nauvoo Temple. However, once the Saints were pushed from Nauvoo, this practice continued. Without a temple, men and women were "welcomed" into leaders' families with the understanding that when a temple was constructed in Utah, the adoption would be solidified.

It's fascinating that Winter Quarters was laid out based on family or "tribal" order. Those adopted to Brigham Young lived in the center of Winter Quarters. Willard Richards' families settled on the east, and the southern blocks of town were occupied by Heber C. Kimball and the families adopted to him. Winter Quarters was structured this way to promote unity. However, as ironic as it might seem, this configuration of the town was one of the first flaws discovered with this practice. Some Saints would brag to others about the family they were adopted into, leading to hard feelings. The arrogance of some Saints caused Brigham Young not to push the principle in the Salt Lake Valley, even though the practice continued.[6]

Another factor causing the principle to die a slow death was that the General Authority had to be present in the temple for the adoption ceremony. Not all General Authorities could be present, depending on missions or other Church assignments.[7] The biggest reason the practice ended was Elder Wilford Woodruff's revelation of the Founding Fathers of this country and their push to have him complete their work. From 1877 to 1894, both as an Apostle and also as President of the church, Wilford pressed to have members research their families, submit their names, and do their temple work, culminating with the sealing ceremony where they could be tied to "their" family, rather than adopted to the family of a General Authority. In 1894, President Woodruff officially ended the practice of adoption.[8] President Woodruff, addressing the temple presidents serving at the time in the Church (President Lorenzo Snow of the Salt Lake Temple, President M. W. Merrill of the Logan Temple, President J. D. T. McAllister of the Manti Temple, and President D. H. Cannon of the St. George Temple), stated that they as temple presidents had, up to this point in time, operated according to the knowledge that they had been given. However, Wilford Woodruff went on to state that there was more than what was currently understood at the time in "turn[ing] the hearts of the fathers to the children, and the children to their fathers" (Malachi 4:5–6). The prophet made it clear that there was additional revelation they were not acting on. President Woodruff was clear when he stated the prophets before him were not comfortable with the principle of adopting members of the Church to General Authorities. He continued that Brigham Young received revelation, and based on this revelation changes were made in the St. George Temple, that revelation has continued which would bring about new changes as far as the sealing ordinance of children to their fathers.

When praying on the subject, the Spirit whispered to Wilford Woodruff, "Have you not a father who begot you?"

"Yes, I have."

"Then why not honor him? Why not be adopted to him?"

"Yes," said I, "that is right."

President Woodruff then instructed that when a man receives his endowment he should be sealed to his father and not to another man outside his lineage. He then finalized what he taught by stating, "This is the will of God to his people."[9]

NOTES

1. *Minutes and Discourse*, 6–8 April 1844, as reported by William Clayton as found in josephsmithspapers.org.
2. Brigham Young, speech, *Times and Seasons* 6 (1845): 953–57.
3. Carl J. Cranney, "Led Just Right," The Theological Development of Vertical Latter-day Saint Sealings through 1894, *Mormon Historical Studies,* Spring 2019, 83.
4. Carl J. Cranney, "Led Just Right," The Theological Development of Vertical Latter-day Saint Sealings through 1894, 86.
5. Jennifer Ann Mackley, *Wilford Woodruff's Witness of the Development of Temple Doctrine* (Seattle, WA: High Desert Publishing, 2014), 33.
6. Harley, William G., ed., *History of the Saints (*American Fork, Utah: Covenant Communications, 2012), 64.
7. Harley, William G., ed., *History of the Saints*, 64.
8. Ibid.
9. Lesson Committee, *Chronicles of Courage* (Salt Lake City: Utah Printing Company, 1995), 6:4–6.

For additional exceptional information on this topic read, Carl J. Cranney, "Led Just Right," The Theological Development of Vertical Latter-day Saint Sealings through 1894, *Mormon Historical Studies,* Spring 2019, 77–110.

Alphabet

As incredible as it may seem, for a period of time the Church trialed the use of a new alphabet, different from the standard English alphabet in use today. Why the change? Maybe you have perplexed over the confused look on your child's face as you have tried to explain the different sounds one letter in the alphabet is capable of creating. Brigham Young also had the same issues with the English language. On one occasion he instructed:

> Brother Spencer has used language quite beyond your reach. Well, I have the foundation, and he can make the building. When he commences the building, I have asked the Board of Regents to cast out from their system of education, the present orthography and written form of our language, that when my children are taught the graphic sign for A, it may always represent that individual sound only. But as it now is, the child is perplexed that the sign A should have one sound in *mate*, a second sound in *father*, a third sound in *fall*, and a fourth sound in *man*, and a fifth sound in *many*, and, in other combinations, sounding different from these, while, in others, A is not sounded at all. I say, let it have one sound all the time. And when P is introduced into a word, let it not be silent as in *Phthisic*, or sound like F in *Physic*, and let two not be placed instead of one in apple.[1]

President Young realized there was a solution. Having attended Pittman shorthand classes in Nauvoo, as taught by British immigrant George Watt, Young realized that this could be the solution.[2] Brigham Young once stated: "We will continue to improve the whole science of truth; for that is our business; our religion circumscribes all things, and we should be prepared to take hold of whatever will be a benefit and blessing to us."[3]

On February 21, 1850, the University of Deseret was incorporated.[4] On March 20, 1850, the Board of Regents that was created at the time of the formation of the University of Deseret met in the home of Parley P. Pratt when a discussion ensued on altering the current English alphabet so "that spelling and Pronunciation should be the same."[5] The January 19, 1854, edition of the *Deseret News* reported:

> The Board of Regents, in company with the Governor and heads of departments, have adopted a new Alphabet, consisting of 38 characters.

> The Board have had frequent sittings this winter, with the sanguine hope of simplifying the English language, and especially its orthography. After many fruitless attempts to render the common alphabet of the day subservient to their purpose, they found it expedient to invent an entirely new and original set of characters.
>
> These characters are much more simple in their structure than the usual alphabetical characters; every superfluous mark supposable, is wholly excluded from them. The written and printed hand are substantially merged in one.
>
> We may derive a hint of the advantage to orthography, from spelling the word *eight*, which in the new alphabet only requires two letters instead of five to spell it, viz: AT. There will be a great saving of time and paper by the use of the new characters; and but a very small part of the time and expense will be requisite in obtaining a knowledge of the language.
>
> The orthography will be so abridged that an ordinary writer can probably write one hundred words a minute with ease, and consequently report the speech of a common speaker without much difficulty.
>
> As soon as this alphabet can be set in type, it will probably be furnished to the schools of the Territory for their use and benefit; not however with a view to immediately supersede the use of the common alphabet—which though it does not make the comers thereunto perfect, still it is a vehicle that has become venerable for age and much hard service.
>
> In the new alphabet every letter has a fixed and unalterable sound; and every word is spelt with reference to given sounds. By this means, strangers can not only acquire a knowledge of our language much more readily, but a practised reporter can also report a strange tongue so that the strange language when spoken can be legible by one conversant with the tongue.[6]

The symbols of the new alphabet appeared on gold coins minted in the Salt Lake Valley in 1860. The symbols from the new alphabet spelled out "Holiness to the Lord." This was soon followed by the same symbols on paper money, store front signs, and believe it or not, tombstones. By 1869, readers were published (the *Deseret First Book* and the *Deseret Second Book)*, designed to educate all people of readable age the new language. Other books printed using the Deseret Alphabet included portions of the Book of Mormon and *A Christmas Carol.*[7]

So why don't we use the Deseret alphabet today? For whatever reason, not all educators in Utah Territory taught the new system. With time interest was lost and by 1870 the idea failed.[8]

NOTES

1. In *Journal of Discourses*, 26 vols. (London: Latter-day Saints' Book Depot, 1854–86), 1:70.
2. See Willard Richards, "Conference Minutes," *Times and Seasons*, April 15, 1845, 871; See Larry Ray Wintersteen, "A History of the Deseret Alphabet" (master's thesis, Brigham Young University, 1970), 17.
3. Bishops' Meetings 1871–79, July 26, 1877, as quoted in Leonard J. Arrington, *Brigham Young: American Moses* (New York: Alfred A. Knopf, 1985), 397.
4. William E. Berrett and Alma P. Burton, *Readings in L.D.S. Church History* (Salt Lake City: Deseret Book, 1967), 2:452.
5. Minutes of the Board of Regents of the Deseret University, March 20, 1850, Utah Territorial Collection, Church Archives, as quoted in Kenneth Reid Beesley, "The Deseret Alphabet: Can Orthographical Reform for English Succeed?" (paper written for Brigham Young University honors program, 1975), 2–3; see also *Diary of Samuel W. Richards*, L. Tom Perry Special Collections, Harold B. Lee Library, Brigham Young University, Provo, UT, 91.
6. "The New Alphabet," *Deseret News*, January 19, 1854.
7. Lawrence R. Flake,*Prophets and Apostles of the Last Dispensation* (Provo, Utah: Religious Study Center, Brigham Young University, 2001), 372–73; Kathryn Jenkins Gordon, *Colorful Characters in Mormon History* (American Fork, Utah: Covenant Communications Inc., 2015), 137–138.; byui.edu/special-collections/deseret-alphabet
8. rsc.byu.edu/vol-7–no-3–2006/deseret-alphabet-experiment#_edn2

For additional information, see rsc.byu.edu/vol-7–no-3–2006/deseret-alphabet-experiment#_edn2

Baby Blessings

In 1845, Phoebe Woodruff gave birth to a son. Phoebe and Wilford blessed the baby when he was eight days old. While Phoebe held the baby, Wilford anointed his young son and offered a blessing.[1] During the blessing, Wilford Woodruff ordained his son a high priest.[2]

Baby blessings continue today. However, as you read the above incident involving Wilford and Phoebe Woodruff, I'm sure you identified three notable changes from the way this was executed to the way it is performed today. First, in the early restored Church, blessing the baby at eight days of age was important because this tied the baby blessing to biblical times when Hebrews circumcised their sons at eight days old. Second, Phoebe held the baby.[3] (I've blessed six of my own children and have seen many of my twenty grandchildren blessed as babies, and never once did my wife, daughters, or daughters-in-law hold the child. Why? Simply because this isn't the current protocol for this ordinance.) And finally, Wilford anointed the child. Again, this is a practice that no longer exists.[4]

Another ritual tied to baby blessings in the early Church that no longer exists since the days of John Taylor was the bishop of the ward pronounced the blessing for the child, even if the baby didn't belong to the bishop.[5] Of course in Joseph Smith's day during the Palmyra and Kirtland years of the Church, wards didn't exist. The only bishops were regional bishops. In this case, the babies were most likely blessed by the elders of the Church as Doctrine and Covenant 20:70 instructs: "Every member of the church of Christ having children is to bring them unto the elders before the church, who are to lay their hands upon them in the name of Jesus Christ, and bless them in his name."

NOTES

1. Jonathan A. Stapley, "Adoptive Sealing Ritual in Mormonism," *The Journal of Mormon History,* Vol. 37, Summer 2011, 58.
2. Scott G. Kenney, ed. *Wilford Woodruff's Journal, 1833–1898,* 9 vols. (Midvale, Utah: Signature Books, 1983–1985) 2:585. See note at the bottom of the page.
3. Stapley, "Adoptive Sealing Ritual in Mormonism," 58.
4. Ibid.
5. Ibid.

For additional reading, see Stapley's book, *The Power of Godliness: Mormon Liturgy and Cosmology.*

Baptisms and Baptismal Fonts

Today, girls and boys are baptized members of the Church either on their eighth birthday or shortly after. This is a big deal in these young people's lives. We excite the kids for this event by teaching and singing during Primary in preparation for this special and sacred ordinance. Of course parents play an important role and devote time discussing this necessary step for salvation with their child in family home evening or during one-on-one time.

Because the Saints lacked indoor facilities to perform eight-year-old baptisms until well into the twentieth century, the baptisms of those who turned of age during the colder months of the year would generally be put off for more congenial temperatures. It wasn't until 1877 that leaders urged parents of children to baptize them on their eighth birthday rather than wait if the child was "afraid of the cold water."[1]

The following comical story told by Rulon Francis Thompson is reminiscent of what it was like for eight-year-old children to be baptized in cold water during the pioneer phase of the Church:

> I was baptized north of [Richmond]. [The area] was all covered with hawthorn bushes and known as Muddy River [and is now called the Cub River]. Several boys were baptized that day. I remember how cold the water was. It took your breath as you waded out into the river to where we were to be immersed. The water came almost up to our shoulders. When one of the boys, LaFayette Tibbets, came up out of the water he said, "Hell, that's cold!" He was immediately immersed in the water again. When he came up the second time, he kept his mouth shut.[2]

A child's baptism doesn't always happen on one's birthday, but rather at the mercy of the one Saturday a month the stake conducts baptisms. Currently, because of the time the stake designates, it could mean that a young boy or girl can wait days or possibly weeks to get baptized after their eighth birthday. However, it appears that during pioneer times and during the Territorial Utah years, young eight-year old Saints could wait months for warmer days.

It's fascinating to learn when the Manti Temple was built and dedicated, the baptismal font was used for a variety of uses other than baptisms for the dead, one of which was eight-year-old baptisms. We perceive the temple baptismal font as a structure dedicated for the work of the dead and not the living.[3] However, when one reads the narrative of Rulon Francis Thompson, it makes perfect sense. To have ice broken in a frozen lake, pond, or creek must been terrifying to some of these young children. Rather than eagerly anticipating their baptism, some may have dreaded it. I can almost imagine the fear of some of the children and the consternation from their mothers as they watched their children enter the frigid water, holding a quilt or two to immediately wrap their child in at the conclusion of the ordinance. I could be wrong, but adding all these worries together and the spirit of the occasion could possibly be constrained for some children and their families. It may be because of winter time baptisms, and the associated concerns created by seasonal temperatures, that the Church leaders justified the use of the Manti Temple baptismal font as an option for those who didn't want to wait for more temperate weather.[4]

This also points to the fact that few baptismal fonts existed in Utah Territory. Had there existed numerous meetinghouses, each one equipped with a baptismal font the way it is today, it's possible that Church leaders may have restricted the use of the temple font for work of the dead only.

The first font dedicated in Utah was in 1856, located near the Endowment House. Imagine the Saints' joy when a year later another baptismal font was dedicated in the Salt Lake City's 14th Ward building. Brigham Young, ever mindful of the Saints' needs, boarded a wagon box approximately ten feet by twelve feet. To add to the comfort, Brigham added dressing rooms that were attached to the font. This was dedicated on September 4, 1861.

In 1875 millwright Frederick Kesler was approached by the presiding bishop to construct a baptismal font. Brother Kesler didn't disappoint. He constructed the font in such a way that the person being baptized would face the east when they were brought out of the water to replicate the resurrection. Frederick Kesler thought since Jesus Christ was baptized in running water (the Jordan River), he would replicate the current of a river and installed water pipes to supply the font.[5]

Long gone are the days of pioneer outdoor baptism. True, there are those today who choose to be nostalgic and, coupled with the bishop's approval, prefer to be baptized in an ocean, lake, or creek. The operative word is "choose." Yes, today we have the choice, a luxury the pioneers lacked. Along with baptisms today is a closet with a ready supply of white baptismal clothes, warm clean water in a font complete with smooth bottom, a warm building, a room furnished with a piano, and a changing room so that after the ordinance has concluded the young boy or girl can remove their wet baptismal clothing and put on their dry Sunday best.

NOTES

1. Ronald W. Walker and Doris R. Dant ed., *Nearly Everything Imaginable* (Provo, Utah: BYU Press, 1999), 270.
2. Susan Arrington, *Growing up in Zion* (Salt Lake City: Deseret Book, 1996), 51.
3. splendidsun.com/wp/baptism-healing/
4. Ibid.
5. Ronald W. Walker and Doris R. Dant ed., *Nearly Everything Imaginable*, 270.

Baptism, Re

For a number of decades the Church practiced what was referred to as re-baptism. The authorities saw this as an opportunity for the Saints to renew their covenants as a rededication or recommitment at important events in their lives. The four most notable events that initiated a re-baptism generally, but not always, occurred whenever an individual entered Utah after a long and arduous journey on the trail west. The second and third common incidents with many of the Saints was during the Church's consecration movement of 1854 and the "Mormon Reformation" between 1856–57. The fourth occurrence was at the time Saints agreed to enter the United Order during the mid-1870s.

It's interesting that in Utah the Quorum of the Twelve set the example first by going into the waters of baptism, initiating this practice. Other occasions, but not as prevalent, were the re-baptism of a disfellowshipped member from the Church, or an individual who committed a serious offense that did not warrant being disfellowshipped but expressed remorse and contrition in their attitude to conform to the laws and principles governing the gospel.[1]

It's intriguing that the prayer for those re-baptized at their admittance into the United Order read different from the formal baptismal prayer one would experience at a convert or eight-year-old baptism. The United Order baptismal prayer read as follows: "Having Authority given me of Jesus Christ, I baptize you for the remission of your Sins, for the renewal of your covenants, and for the Observance of the Rules of the Holy United Order in the Name of the Father, Son and Holy Ghost. Amen." The confirmation followed.[2]

As I've read various Church history sources by various authors, I've bumped into other occasions when the principle of re-baptism was practiced. The following is from the William White family:

> As we wished to go and work in the Temple and it was council for all to get baptized before going. . . I was adopted to my Father and Mother. . . This labor was a great comfort to us. . . We received our second Washings and anointing. They said as we were coming a way so far we could receive them but they never had given them to any one so young. . . . We were in Heaven sure when we were working in that Holy place but when we get out Stan doubles his force on a person trying to make up for the good one receives.[3]

When and why did this practice end? During the October 1897 general conference, George Q. Cannon, speaking to the assembled Saints, stated that too many members of the Church saw this as an easy way to repent.[4]

NOTES

1. Ronald W. Walker and Doris R. Dant ed., *Nearly Everything Imaginable (*Provo, Utah: BYU Press, 1999), 271.
2. Leonard J. Arrington and David Bitton, *Saints Without Halos* (Salt Lake City: Signature Books, 1982), 68.
3. Ibid., 73, 77.
4. James B. Allen and Glen M. Leonard, *The Story of the Latter-day Saints,* 2d ed. (Salt Lake City: Deseret Book, 1992), 430–431.

Baptism for Healing

It may seem odd to us today, but it commonly occurred for people suffering from adverse effects of sickness or other bodily ailments to be baptized for healing during the Nauvoo years, to Winter Quarters, and on through to Utah. In fact, this practice continued well into the twentieth century. What made it more peculiar is both member and non-members benefitted from this practice. Thomas L. Kane, a non-member friend to the Saints, was seriously ill and dying from the effects of malaria while residing with members of the Church at Winter Quarters. Like many of the Saints during this period of time in Church history, Major Kane was baptized for healing.[1]

When and how did this practice begin? In an October 12 [1841] epistle designed to encourage members to finish the temple, the Twelve wrote:

> The time has come when the great Jehovah would have a resting place on earth, a habitation for his chosen, where his law shall be revealed, and his servants be endued from on high, to bring together the honest in heart from the four winds; where the saints may enter the Baptismal Font for their dead relations . . . a place, over which the heavenly messengers may watch and trouble the waters as in days of old, so that when the sick are put therein they shall be made whole.[2]

It appears the first actual healing occurred less than a month later after the Quorum of the Twelve's epistle to the Saints. As interesting as it may seem, the Quorum of the Twelve did not mention the actual method as a "baptism" for healing, but rather, like biblical times, "the troubling of the waters." On November 8, 1841, William Clayton recorded Joseph Smith's instructions to Samuel Rolfe to wash in the wooden baptismal font in the Nauvoo Temple.

"Brother Samuel Rolfe being present, and being seriously afflicted with a felon on one hand president Joseph instructed him to wash in the font, and told him he would be healed, although the doctors had told him it would not be well before spring, and advised him to have it cut. He washed his hands in the font and in one week afterwards his hand was perfectly healed."[3]

The following is found in *The Joseph Smith Papers:* "In February 1842 Samuel Rolfe washed his hands in the Font being seriously affected with a Fellon, so that the Docters thought it ought to be cut open; others said it would not be well before spring. After washing in the Font his hand healed in one week."[4]

Joseph Smith was all about religious tolerance. On a number of occasions ministers of other faiths were permitted to speak from the stand in the grove to the Saints during Sunday worship services. Knowing the Prophet Joseph was this comfortable with ministers of other denominations mingling among the Saints in Nauvoo, it's little wonder he would also invite these gentlemen to tour the holy edifice. The Reverend George Moore was one such minister who visited the unfinished Nauvoo Temple, expressing the following after the tour: "In the basement is the baptismal font, supported by 12 oxen. In this I learned that persons are baptized for the dead, and for restoration to health."[5]

In the April 1842 general conference, Joseph Smith instructed: "Baptisms for the dead, and for the healing of the body must be in the font, those coming into the Church, and those re-baptized may be baptized in the river."[6]

At some point between Brother Rolfe's dipping his hand into the water of the Nauvoo Temple baptismal font and the following experience shared by Bathsheba Smith in a letter to her husband, Elder George A. Smith, on October 2, 1842, this practice evolved to the actual physical baptism of the sick individual:

> George Albert was sick last Saturday and Sunday. He had quite a fever. I was very uneasy about him. I was afraid he was going to have the fever. I took him to the font and had him baptized and since then he has not had any fever. He is about well now. Looks a little pale. I anointed him with oil a good may times and washed his little body with whisky and water which was burning with fever but it did not do the good I wanted it should.[7]

Was it necessary to perform baptisms for healings inside the temple only? It is recorded that Joseph Smith preformed this for his sick wife, Emma, in the Mississippi River on October 5, 1842, and a second time on November 1, 1842.[8]

This practice came to an end in 1922 with a letter to temple presidents from the First Presidency with this announcement:

> We feel constrained to call your attention to the custom prevailing to some extent in our temples of baptizing for health, and to remind you that baptism for health is no part of our temple work, and therefore to permit it to become a practice would be an innovation detrimental to temple work, and a departure as well from the provision instituted of the Lord for the care and healing of the sick of His Church.[9]

NOTES

1. David J. Whittaker, "New Sources on Old Friends: The Thomas L. Kane and Elizabeth W. Kane Collection," *Journal of Mormon History 27* (Spring 2001), 67–94.
2. Brigham Young et al., "An Epistle of the Twelve, Nauvoo, October 12, 1841," Times and Seasons 2 (October 15, 1841): 569.
3. *Journal of William Clayton*, 1840–1845, 21, 8 November 1841, Church Archives.
4. Josephsmithspapers.org, 127.
5. George Moore Diary (1982)*Western Illinois Regional Studies* vol. 5, 6.
6. Joseph Smith, *Times and Seasons* vol. 3 no. 12, 763; *HC* 4:586 & 7:358.
7. Kenneth W. Godfrey, Audrey M. Godfrey, Jill Mulvay Derr, *Women's Voices-An Untold History of The Latter-day Saints 1830–1900* (Salt Lake City: Deseret Book, 1982), 122–23.
8. D. Michael Quinn (1978), "The Practice of Rebaptism at Nauvoo," *BYU Studies*, vol. 18, 230.
9. *Messages of the First Presidency of The Church of Jesus Christ of Latter-day Saints*, vol. 5, 224.

For additional information on the Thomas L. Kane situation, see Matthew Grow, *"Liberty to the Downtrodden": Thomas L. Kane, Romantic Reformer* (New Haven, Connecticut: Yale University Press, 2009).

Baptism for the Dead

A glorious vision of the celestial kingdom was bestowed upon Joseph Smith in January 1836 wherein Joseph discovered that those who had passed on without receiving the gospel, like his brother Alvin, "would not be denied the highest rewards in the life to come." This vision was the opening for further light and knowledge on the doctrines in relation to baptism for the dead that both Joseph Smith and his successors would continue to receive for the next several years.[1]

Since August 15, 1840, during the funeral sermon of Seymour Brunso, when Joseph Smith first introduced the principle of being baptized for one's own ancestors, we as Latter-day Saints have practiced baptisms for the dead through the decades to today. What was noteworthy about this day was immediately after the funeral concluded, a sister by the name of Jane Neyman entered the Mississippi River and was baptized for her deceased son, Cyrus, by Brother Harvey Olmstead and witnessed by Vienna Jacques while Vienna was sitting on her horse in the Mississippi River.[2]

In its almost 180–year history, there have been changes to the way the ordinance was originally performed. Reading the Neyman/Olmstead baptism, I'm positive you may have identified three differences from the way we currently perform baptisms for the dead. First, during the Nauvoo years, women could be baptized for men and vice versa. Second, the ordinance was first performed in rivers until the font could be dedicated in the Nauvoo Temple, regardless of the fact that the remainder of the temple was far from completion. The font at this time was in the basement of the temple with a temporary roof as a covering. Third, the witness was Vienna Jacques, a sister. Until recently, only men were allowed to serve as witnesses. Now, under a recent change, men and women can serve as witnesses as they did in Nauvoo.

In September 1840, as Joseph Smith Sr. lay dying, his prophet-son explained the principle of baptism for the dead. The Prophet explained to his father that Alvin, who seven years prior to the Church being organized passed away, could now have this ordinance performed. Joseph Sr. directed Joseph to take care of this immediately and asked that Joseph Jr. act as the proxy for his brother.[3] A record has never materialized of when Alvin Smith had this work accomplished for him. It is thought that it was performed shortly after Joseph Smith Sr. died during September of 1840. What's compelling is once the font in the temple was dedicated, Alvin's baptism was performed a second time in 1841. In fact, Joseph Smith instructed those who had baptized ancestors for the dead in the Mississippi River to repeat this ordinance in the Nauvoo Temple font.[4]

You might have also detected from the story of Jane Neyman the absence of the confirmation blessing at the conclusion of the baptism. It's possible that this could have taken place; however, the record is silent.

In 1873 Brigham Young stood at the pulpit and noticed a number of the "old Saints" who lived during the time the Church was centered in Nauvoo. He reminded these Saints of the time when the Prophet Joseph Smith first received revelation pertaining "to how the dead could be officiated for," that sisters were baptized for their male relatives and ancestors as were the brethren baptized for female individuals in their families. President Young continued to recap the practice during the Nauvoo years by telling the Saints that there wasn't much given in the practices of baptism for the dead, but with time more revelation came. He also stated that at first no record was kept, but eventually Joseph Smith taught that records are to be taken when he confirmed to the female Relief Society on August 31, 1842: "All persons baptized for the dead must have a recorder present, that he may be an eyewitness to record and testify of the truth and validity of his record. It will be necessary, in the Grand Council, that these things be testified."[5]

The following day, in a letter to the Saints, Joseph explained the necessity for a recorder when he instructed: "That in all your recordings, it may be recorded in heaven. . . . And again, let all the records be had in order, that they may be put in the archives of my Holy Temple, to be held in remembrance from generation to generation, saith the Lord of Hosts."[6]

This letter is now section 127 in the Doctrine and Covenants. You have to know the concern Joseph Smith believed for the records of such baptisms when he wrote a second letter to the Saints, dated September 7, 1842, wherein again he instructed the records of baptisms for the dead, along with witnesses at the performance of the baptisms.[7]

Charlotte Haven, a non-member who lived in Nauvoo for a few months, wrote the following letter to family members in the East. The letter is dated May 2, 1843:

Last Sunday morning . . . was a balmy spring day, so we took a bee-line for the river, down the street north of our house. Arriving there we rested a while on a log, watching the thin sheets of ice as they slowly came down and floated by. Then we followed the bank toward town, and rounding a little point covered with willows and cottonwoods, we spied quite a crowd of people, and soon perceived there was a baptism. Two elders stood knee- deep in the ice cold water, and immersed one another as fast as they could come down the bank. We soon observed that some of them went in and were plunged several times. We were told that they were baptized for the dead who had not had an opportunity of adopting the doctrines of the Latter Day Saints. So these poor mortals in ice-cold water were releasing their ancestors and relatives from purgatory! We drew a little nearer and heard several names repeated by the elders as the victims were douched, and you can imagine our surprise when the name George Washington was called. So after these fifty years he is out of purgatory and on his way to the 'celestial' heaven! It was enough and we continued our walk homeward.[8]

NOTES

1. churchofjesuschrist.org/study/manual/revelations-in-context/letters-on-baptism-for-the-dead?lang=eng
2. Jane Neyman statement, given Nov. 29, 1854, in *Journal History*, Aug. 15, 1840.
3. *History of the Church* 4:179.
4. "Nauvoo Baptisms for the Dead," Book A, Church Genealogical Society Archives, 45, 149.
5. Joseph Smith in *History of the Church* 5:141; *Journal of Discourses*, v. 16, pp. 165–66.
6. churchofjesuschrist.org/study/manual/revelations-in-context/letters-on-baptism-for-the-dead?lang=eng; Doctrine and Covenants, 1844 ed., 419–20, josephsmithpapers.org.
7. churchofjesuschrist.org/study/manual/revelations-in-context/letters-on-baptism-for-the-dead?lang=eng; Joseph Smith, "Journal, December 1841–December 1842."
8. San Francisco *Overland Monthly,* Vol. 16, December 1890, No. 96.

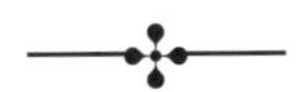

Birth and Relief Society Participation

The birth of a child is an exciting time for a family, a time when the father can exercise his priesthood power and provide a blessing of comfort for his wife shortly before she delivers the welcomed new member into the home. Giving a priesthood blessing is what we've grown accustomed to in modern times. However, even though I suppose fathers have always exercised this power through the decades, surprisingly it was not uncommon for the Relief Society sisters to wash and anoint fellow sisters about to give birth during the early Utah Territory years.[1] Sister Tenn Young, at an 1896 Relief Society conference in the Logan Tabernacle, stated: "I wish to speak of the great privilege given to us to wash and anoint the sick and suffering of our sex. I would counsel everyone who expects to become a Mother to have these ordinances administered by some good faithful sister."[2]

In her article in the *Journal of Mormon History*, Susanna Morrill shares the following:

> As a result of these hard realities and the resulting fears, Relief Society members, as well as male priesthood holders, would often bless expectant mothers before childbirth. Relief Society women took an active role in attempting to stabilize these joyful but dangerous times of birth, providing reassurance and comfort with overtly religious rituals. As Linda King Newell has shown, the practice by women seems to have often involved a detailed ritual of washing the expectant mother in water while speaking blessings and then repeating the process with consecrated oil. These blessings bear formal similarity to washings, anointings, and blessings performed during temple ceremonies.[3]

In 1888 Emmeline B. Wells wrote Wilford Woodruff questions pertaining to the propriety of the practice. The following are her questions complete with Wilford Woodruff's response:

> First: Are sisters justified in administering the ordinance of washing and anointing previous to confinements [child birth] to those who have received their endowments and have married men outside of the Church? Second: Can anyone who has not had their endowments thus

be administered to by the sisters if she is a faithful Saint in good standing and has not yet had the opportunity of going to the temple for the ordinances?

Wilford Woodruff's answer:

> To begin with I desire to say that the ordinance of washing and anointing is one that should only be administered in Temples or other holy places which are dedicated for the purpose of giving endowments to the Saints. That ordinance might not be administered to any one whether she has received or has not received her endowments, in any other place or under any other circumstances. But I imagine from your questions that you refer to a practice that has grown up among the sisters of washing and anointing sisters who are approaching their confinement. If so, this is not, strictly speaking, an ordinance, unless it be done under the direction of the priesthood and in connection with the ordinance of laying on of hands for the restoration of the sick. There is no impropriety in sisters washing and anointing their sisters in this way, under the circumstances you describe; but it should be understood that they do this, not as members of the priesthood, but as members of the Church, exercising faith for, and asking the blessings of the Lord upon, their sisters, just asking the blessings of the Lord upon their sisters, just as they and every member of the Church, might do in behalf of the members of their families.[4]

On July 29, 1946, Joseph Fielding Smith of the Quorum of the Twelve sent a letter to Belle S. Spafford, the general Relief Society president, in which the practice of women washing and anointing prior to child birth came to an end. A portion of the letter read: "While the authorities of the Church have ruled that it is permissible, under certain conditions and with the approval of the priesthood, for sisters to wash and anoint other sisters, yet they feel that it is far better for us to follow the plan the Lord has given us and send for the Elders of the Church to come and administer to the sick and afflicted."[5]

NOTES

1. Reid L. Neilson and Ronald W. Walker, *Reflections of A Mormon Historian-Leonard J. Arrington on the New Mormon History (*Norman, Oklahoma: The Arthur H. Clark Company, 2006), 213.
2. Cache Valley Stake Relief Society Minute Book B, 11 Sept. 1886, 4648, Church Archives.

3. Susanna Morrill, "Relief Society Birth and Death, Rituals: Women at the Gates of Mortality," *The Journal of Mormon History,* Spring 2010, 145–46.
4. History of the Church, volume 4, 604.
5. Quoted in Messages of the First Presidency, 4:314

For additional detail into this practice, see Susanna Morrill, "Relief Society Birth and Death, Rituals: Women at the Gates of Mortality," *The Journal of Mormon History,* Spring 2010.

Bishops

According to the Church website, "The office of bishop was one of the first priesthood offices restored in this dispensation, and, like other offices, an understanding of the duties of a bishop came line upon line."[1]

Today bishops serve for approximately five years. However, during pioneer times, after five years, a bishop was barely broken in. Trust me, when called to serve as "father of the ward" in Utah Territory, one could count on being in for the long haul. Elijah Sheets presently holds the record for longevity, having served as the ward ecclesiastical leader for forty-eight years. It's interesting that three weeks after his release on June 12, 1904, he passed away.[2] However, to be fair, the bishops of today must manage the entire program of the Church with the associated auxiliaries, whereas this wasn't always the case of bishops in pre-1870 Utah Territory.

It's remarkable that not all bishops called in the early days of Utah Territory were married as Paul, of New Testament fame, indicated is a stipulation. Surprised, Orson Ferguson Whitney was ordained to be the bishop of the Eighteenth Ward in Salt Lake City. After presented and receiving the sustain vote, the stake president said to all sitting in the stake meeting, "Paul says that a Bishop must be the husband of one wife; it is to be hoped that Bishop Whitney will soon qualify."[3] George W. Tolley found himself at age twenty-one in the same shocking situation when called to be the bishop of the Orton (Utah) Ward. Again, he was unmarried, yet called to serve.

Here are some other interesting facts surrounding bishops serving in Utah Territory. Even though the reasoning is unclear, in 1868, all bishops in the Weber Stake (Utah) were released, with the exception of Chauncey W. West, who served as the lone bishop in the stake.[4]

Some bishops did double duty, called to serve simultaneously in other time-consuming callings while acting as the ecclesiastical leader of their ward. One such bishop was Edwin Dilworth Woolley Sr. In 1853, he was called as bishop of the Salt Lake 13th Ward, then later sustained in a dual capacity in the Tabernacle during general conference on April 7, 1854, to serve in his stake high council, a position he held many years.[5]

Other obligations of Bishop Woolley's during his tenure, that bishops most likely never heard of today, were ensuring the ward school continued to run efficiently and that the ward fence was in place and repaired.[6] Ward fence? Yes, believe it or not, ward boundaries were not determined by virtual lines but by the physical presence of a fence. I'm sure most members of the Church have been involved with at least one interesting ward boundary. I recall years ago when ward boundaries were realigned in our stake. One ward lacked the priesthood leadership it required to be successful. To remedy the issue the stake drew a virtual line nine-tenths of a mile from the western boundary of this ward, down Morley Ave. into the neighboring ward, circled the house of the desired leader, and then back to the original boundary. I would love to have seen that ward fence.

As strange as it may seem, bishops didn't always reside in their ward boundaries. In a sense this continues today when men are called to serve in singles wards and MTC branches. The difference between today and those called during the Utah Territorial years is the length of the call. Today it is generally for five years. However, as mentioned earlier, the Utah Territory bishops could serve for decades. Bishop Elijah F. Sheets is a prime example. Called in 1856 to the Eighth Ward in Salt Lake City, he eventually moved to Provo to serve in the stake presidency under Abraham O. Smoot but was never released as bishop in the Eighth Ward. Even at the time of Brother Sheets' release in 1904, he was not living in his ward boundary. While he was serving a genealogical mission to Pennsylvania from 1869–70, one would assume he qualified for a release. Not so. He continued to serve as both bishop and missionary simultaneously.[7]

Today, if a member of The Church of Jesus Christ of Latter-day Saints violates a municipal, state, or federal law, the individual is treated like any other person, regardless of race or creed, and tried by the courts of the land. Nonetheless, it wasn't always like this in the earliest days of Utah. To be honest, when you think about it, it couldn't. It's the way it had to be, at least for a time. It's compelling to think of the bishops and high council in early-day Utah as both the judge and jury not only in spiritual, church-related matters, but also with everyday municipal and state of Deseret law. Nevertheless, as mentioned, this is the way it had to be, since the only whites in the valley for the first few years were members of the Church (with the exception of a handful of trappers and mountain men). Since the Church leadership was not trained in the laws of the land (university education), the question might be asked, just how reasonable were these secular courts? At first, at least until 1849 (this type of government lasted from July 1847 to March 1849), when the first gold seekers were on their journey to the California gold fields, those breaking the laws of the land were the Saints and maybe a few desperadoes. I'm sure in these cases it was easy since the Saints were already accustomed to Church courts, whether this was at a ward or stake level. However, when the gentile population mingled with the Saints, I imagine things became interesting to observe how these cases would be handled.

Two early non-member visitors to the Utah area were Captain Stansbury and Lieutenant Gunnison. Stansbury shares his thoughts on the Church's judicial system:

> The jurisdiction of the State of Deseret had been extended over and was vigorously enforced upon all who came within its borders, and justice was equitably administered alike to 'saints' and 'gentiles'—as they term all who are not of their persuasions. . . .
>
> Their courts were constantly appealed to by companies of passing emigrants, who, having fallen out by the way, could not agree upon the division of their property. The decisions were remarkable for fairness and impartiality, and, if not submitted to, were sternly enforced by the whole power of the community.[8]

It is said that Daniel Spencer, an early stake president in Salt Lake City, was extremely fair to both Saint and Gentile. The story is told of a bishop from the St. George area, many thousands of dollars in debt to a Salt Lake City banker, a Mr. Noonan. Mr. Noonan took the complaint to President Spencer. A court was held and at the end of the trial, after arguments were heard on both sides, the stake council ruled in favor of Mr. Noonan. The St. George bishop was asked to pay the full amount to Mr. Noonan in twenty-eight days or lose his title as bishop. Mr. Noonan, ever so grateful for the equity in which the trial was handled, offered money to the stake council. This was appreciated, but declined since these courts were free of charge.[9]

NOTES

1. churchofjesuschrist.org/study/manual/revelations-in-context/a-bishop-unto-the-church?lang=eng
2. Skousen, Paul, *The Skousen Book of Mormon World Records* (Springville, Utah: Cedar Fort, Inc., 2004), 228.
3. Andrew Jenson, *L.D.S Biographical Encyclopedia* (Salt Lake City: Publishers Press, 1901) Vol. 1, 677–78.
4. Andrew Jensen, *LDS Biographical Encyclopedia* (Salt Lake City: Western Epics, 1971), 3:601.
5. International Society Daughters of Utah Pioneers, Museum Memories (Salt Lake City, Utah: Talon Printing, 2011), 3:316.
6. Leonard J. Arrington and David Bitton, *Saints Without Halos* (Salt Lake City: Signature Books, 1982), 56.
7. Donald Q. Cannon and David J. Whittaker, *Supporting Saints: Life Stories of Nineteenth-Century Mormons* (Salt Lake City: Bookcraft Inc., 1985), 256.
8. *Chronicles of Courage,* Lesson Committee (Salt Lake City: Talon Printing, 1996) Vol. 7, 60–61.
9. Andrew Jenson, *LDS Biographical Encyclopedia* (Salt Lake City: Publishers Press, 1901) 1:289.

Book of Mormon

Joseph Smith said that the Book of Mormon was "the most correct of any Book on earth & the keystone of our religion & a man would get nearer to God by abiding by its precepts than by any other Book."[1] And it is. Millions of people the world over have entered the waters of baptism after reading and developing a testimony of the truthfulness of this book of scripture. Through the years, the Book of Mormon has experienced changes in format and punctuation.

The original manuscript, the manuscript that scribes copied as Joseph Smith gave the translation of the gold plates, "includes errors that suggest the scribe heard words incorrectly"[2] For instance: "When Joseph translated the text that is now in 1 Nephi 13:29, the scribe wrote '&' in one place where he should have written 'an.' At 1 Nephi 17:48, the scribe wrote 'weed' where he should have written 'reed.'[3]

Prior to publication, Oliver Cowdery copied from the original manuscript into what is currently known as the printer's manuscript. The fact that Joseph Smith did not include punctuation such as "periods, commas, or question marks, as he dictated,"[4] and since punctuation currently exists in our copies of the Book of Mormon, this indicates there was a change. It might surprise you that the person responsible for inserting the punctuation was not a member of our church, but rather the typesetter for E. B. Grandin, the individual responsible for printing the original Book of Mormon.

The following interesting account from John H. Gilbert, the typesetter for the Book of Mormon, explains how the punctuation happened to be inserted:

> I am a practical printer by trade. I have been a resident of Palmyra, New York, since about the year 1824, and during all that time have done some typesetting each year. I was aged ninety years on the 13th day of April 1892, and on that day I went to the office of the Palmyra Courier and set a stickful of type.
>
> My recollection of past events, and especially of the matters connected with the printing of the "Mormon Bible" [Book of Mormon], is very accurate and faithful, and I have made the following memorandum at request, to accompany the photographs of 'Mormon Hill,' which have been made for the purpose of exhibits at the World's Fair in 1893.
>
> In the forepart of June, 1829, Mr. E. [Egbert] B. Grandin, the printer of the Wayne Sentinel, came to me and said he wanted I should assist him in estimating the cost of printing 5,000 copies of a book that Martin Harris wanted to get printed, which was called the 'Mormon Bible.' It was the second application of Harris to Grandin to do the job—Harris assuring Grandin that the book would be printed in Rochester if he declined the job again.

Harris proposed to have Grandin do the job, if he would, as it would be quite expensive to keep a man in Rochester during the printing of the book, who would have to visit Palmyra two or three times a week for manuscript, etc. Mr. Grandin consented to do the job if his terms were accepted.

A few pages of the manuscript were submitted as a specimen of the whole, and it was said there would be about 500 pages.

The size of the page was agreed upon, and an estimate of the number of ems in a page, which would be 1,000, and that a page of manuscript would make more than a page of printed matter, which proved to be correct.

The contract was to print, and bind with leather, 5,000 copies for $3,000. Mr. Grandin got a new font of small pica, on which the body of the work was printed.

When the printer was ready to commence work, [Martin] Harris was notified, and Hyrum Smith brought the first installment of manuscript, of 24 pages, closely written on common foolscap paper—he had it under his vest, and vest and coat closely buttoned over it. At night [Hyrum] Smith came and got the manuscript, and with the same precaution carried it away. The next morning with the same watchfulness, he brought it again, and at night took it away. This was kept up for several days. The title page was first set up, and after proof was read and corrected, several copies were printed for Harris and his friends. On the second day—[Martin] Harris and [Hyrum] Smith being in the office—I called their attention to a grammatical error, and asked whether I should correct it? [Martin] Harris consulted with [Hyrum] Smith a short time, and turned to me and said, "The Old Testament is ungrammatical, set it as it is written.

After working a few days, I said to [Hyrum] Smith on his handing me the manuscript in the morning, "Mr. [Hyrum] Smith, if you would leave this manuscript with me, I would take it home with me at night and read and punctuate it, and I could get along faster in the daytime, for now I have frequently to stop and read half a page to find how to punctuate it." His reply was, "We are commanded not to leave it." A few mornings after this, when [Hyrum] Smith handed me the manuscript, he said to me, "If you will give your word that this manuscript shall be returned to us when you get through with it, I will leave it with you." I assured Smith that it should be returned all right when I got through with it. For two or three nights I took it home with me and read it, and punctuated it with a lead pencil. This will account for the punctuation marks in pencil, which is referred to in the Mormon Report, an extract from which will be found below.[5]

The Book of Mormon wasn't always arranged into chapters and verses the way we read it presently. In fact, it looked much the same as any book we would read today. In 1879, Orson Pratt undertook the challenge to divide the narrative into verse and chapters. In 1920, the structure of the Book of Mormon was altered again when double columned pages were first introduced. It was during this year when Elder James E. Talmage, heading a committee, added the chapter headings that you currently find in your Book of Mormon, in addition to footnote references, an index, and chronological dates.

What might be less known among members of the Church at present is the Testimony of the Three Witnesses wasn't always located within the first few pages, where we read it today. Note where John Corrill located the Testimony of the Three Witnesses:

> In the course of two or three days, the Book of Mormon (the Golden Bible, as the people then termed it, on account of its having been translated from the Golden plates,) was presented to me for perusal. I looked at it, examined the testimony of the witnesses at the last end of it, read promiscuously a few pages, and made up my mind that it was published for speculation.[6]

Our current book, in the first few pages, has a title page, an introduction, the testimony of various witnesses, including that of Joseph Smith, and an explanation of the Book of Mormon. However, it lacks the original preface that appeared in 1830, which read as follows:

> To the Reader—
>
> As many false reports have been circulated respecting the following work, and also many unlawful measures taken by evil designing persons to destroy me, and also the work, I would inform you that I translated, by the gift and power of God, and caused to be written, one hundred and sixteen pages, the which I took from the Book of Lehi, which was an account abridged from the plates of Lehi, by the hand of Mormon; which said account, some person or persons have stolen and kept from me, notwithstanding my utmost exertions to recover it again—and being commanded of the Lord that I should not translate the same over again, for Satan had put it into their hearts to tempt the Lord their God, by altering the words, that they did read contrary from that which I translated and caused to be written; and if I should bring

forth the same words again, or, in other words, if I should translate the same over again, they would publish that which they had stolen, and Satan would stir up the hearts of this generation, that they might not receive this work: but behold, the Lord said unto me, I will not suffer that Satan shall accomplish his evil design in this thing: therefore thou shalt translate from the plates of Nephi, until ye come to that which ye have translated, which ye have retained; and behold ye shall publish it as the record of Nephi; and thus I will confound those who have altered my words. I will not suffer that they shall destroy my work; yea, I will shew unto them that my wisdom is greater than the cunning of the Devil. Wherefore, to be obedient unto the commandments of God, I have, through his grace and mercy, accomplished that which he hath commanded me respecting this thing. I would also inform you that the plates of which hath been spoken, were found in the township of Manchester, Ontario county, New-York.

The Author.[7]

NOTES

1. Wilford Woodruff journal, Nov. 28, 1841, Church History Library, Salt Lake City in churchofjesuschrist.org/study/manual/gospel-topics essays/book-of-mormon-translation?lang=eng
2. Royal Skousen, "Translating the Book of Mormon: Evidence from the Original Manuscript," in Noel B. Reynolds, ed., *Book of Mormon Authorship Revisited: The Evidence for Ancient Origins*)Provo, UT: Foundation for Ancient Research and Mormon Studies, 1997); in churchofjesuschrist.org/study/manual/gospel-topics-essays/book-of-mormon-translation?lang=eng
3. Royal Skousen, "Translating the Book of Mormon: Evidence from the Original Manuscript," in Noel B. Reynolds, ed., in churchofjesuschrist.org/study/manual/gospel-topics-essays/book-of-mormon-translation?lang=eng
4. Richard E. Turley Jr. and William W. Slaughter, *How We Got the Book of Mormon* (Salt Lake City: Deseret Book, 2011), 44–45 in churchofjesuschrist.org/study/manual/gospel-topics-essays/book-of-mormon-translation?lang=eng
5. Recollections of John H. Gilbert [regarding printing Book of Mormon], 8 September 1892, Palmyra, New York, typescript, BYU; boap.org/
6. John Corrill, *A Brief History of the Church of Christ of Latter Day Saints* (Commonly Called Mormons, Including an Account of their Doctrine and Discipline, with the Reasons of the Author for Leaving the Church) (St. Louis, n.p., 1839).

7. Preface to the Book of Mormon, josephsmithpapers.org/paper-summary/book-of-mormon-1830/9

For additional excellent information see Richard E. Turley Jr and William Slaughter, *How We Got the Book of Mormon* (Salt Lake City: Deseret Book, 2011)

Callings

If there are more people than callings (I'm sure any bishop's dream), then some bishops and their counselors can become creative. I initially discovered this during my first year of college while attending a student singles ward in the institute building at the University of Alberta. Because the Primary simply doesn't exist in singles wards, there were more students available in comparison to the actual number of callings needed to operate the ward. Our bishop was certain to give all a calling, even if some callings were passing out the hymn books prior to and collecting them at the end of the meetings, or setting up and taking down chairs. A sister was called to provide a floral arrangement to enhance the pulpit.

Early bishops in Utah Territory faced much the same challenge. It wasn't until the 1870s that the organization of the ward began to show glimpses of similarity to today's wards. Prior to this there were few callings. Most wards consisted of the bishop, his counselors, a few ward teachers, and a few acting deacons. Most members of the Church simply didn't experience a calling in a ward organization or auxiliary until well into the 1860s. This was all right, though, especially when the Saints first entered the valley. If there was a lack of ward callings, there was plenty of opportunity to establish a community, and since the Saints were the only people on hand to establish a community, who better for the bishops to call to secular type functions?

For instance, during the 1860s a telegraph system found its way to Utah. The territory lacked people with skill to operate such a system.

What better calling to give to the youth?[1] We do the same today. When it comes to higher technical stuff (generally related to various genealogy software programs), who better to train than the youth? And trust me, in those years, telegraphy was high-tech. In 1866, Brigham Young sent William Bryan to train three young ladies (Elizabeth Parks, Hetty Page and Mary Neff) called by their ward bishop in Nephi, Utah, to learn telegraphy.[2]

A new community requires wood to build homes and businesses. What do you do if you don't have lumber men in the community? Again, no problem—you call one. Joel H. Johnson, author of the hymn "High on a Mountain Top," was called to cut lumber for the "building up of Zion." Joel still was required to provide for his family, and since there was little money, he cut a deal with the bishop. He supplied the tithing yard with freshly cut lumber, and in turn he could enter the storehouse and pick out what he required for his family's survival in lieu of wages.[3]

Clearly, the community would require nurses, so it was not uncommon for women to receive callings to serve in such positions in the community. But why stop at nurses? Women in the valley had babies. Who in the Church community could deliver children into the world? It was never an issue. Who better suited to call than members of the Relief Society? It's mentioned that Willard Richards called women "to act as midwives and also administering to the sick and afflicted and set them apart for this very office and calling, and blest them with power to officiate in that capacity as handmaids of the Lord."[4]

The following is from the journal of Jesse N. Smith dated July 1, 1883: "I ordained Warren R. Tenney a High Priest and a High Councilor to fill a vacancy in the High Council. I also set apart Emma S. Smith as president of the Relief Societies of our Stake and Elizabeth Swapp a nurse of the sick."[5]

Those called in the pioneer Church to train as midwives, nurses, and doctors came at a sacrifice on the part of their families. Sarah Jane Veach Lewis tells of a time when Eliza R. Snow visited Richmond in hopes of recruiting sisters capable of developing the skills of midwifery, skills after once attained by attending a course in Salt Lake City would benefit the Richmond, Utah community. Sarah Lewis and Sarah Durney were selected. The selection process didn't sit well with Sister

Lewis. She was irked by what she saw as others in a better situation to leave, advocating her nomination, and yet she had nine children. In her own words she states that she decided to have "a heart to heart" with Brigham Young. President Young wisely, silently listened to Sarah's concerns and then very Brigham-like said to her: "Sister Lewis, I will give you my blessing. You will stay here the allotted time; study, your children will be well and happy during your absence. You shall be blessed in your work. When you have a difficult case, call on me. I promise to be with you. And above all things, have faith."[6]

What about doctors? Yes, the Church community required nurses and midwives, but it also demanded doctors. The Church leaders realized this and set apart such individuals as Martha Hughes Cannon and others to attend medical school. As mentioned above, this came at a huge sacrifice. In many cases these women covered the cost of their own medical school expenses. The other concern that added pressure on the families of the women sent for medical training was, who would take care of the their children during the mother's absence? Obviously, the community would be called (not an actual Church calling) to rally around the family and make certain their needs were met while Mom was away gaining the skills necessary to function as a doctor. Martha graduated in 1880 from the University of Michigan Medical School and later from the University of Pennsylvania.[7] It's interesting that Brigham Young considered the Saints training their own doctors based on his attitude toward those in this profession. It is said that President Young was not a fan of politicians, lawyers, or doctors (not necessarily in that order). I'm sure we understand where Brigham stood with his lack of respect for lawyers and politicians. From day one of the organization of the Church, up to and including the Saints being driven to Utah, in addition to the persecutions during the Utah Territorial years, the history of the Church could fill volumes from the blunders of prejudiced politicians and lawyers. I'm sure Brigham understood those handpicked by the leaders for medical training, companioned with enhanced common sense as directed by the Spirit, would be an asset to the Church community.

The Church also required individuals to take care of the dead. This too was a calling. Much of this load was shouldered by the Relief Society. However, Joseph Smith called Elijah Abel to serve as an undertaker during the Nauvoo years of the Church.[8]

Stake presidents serving during the 1800s were considered fair game when it came to no prior knowledge of their upcoming calling. A prime example is the call of Edwin Dilworth Woolley Jr. to serve as a stake president over the Kanab Stake. One of Brother Woolley's children shares the following story:

> In June of 1884, the Kanab Stake Conference was held in Orderville, Utah, with Erastus Snow representing the general authorities. Father was out on the range at the spring round-up when . . . a runner [was sent] out to bring him in. He had been on the range for three weeks or more and had no clothes except those he had marked and branded cattle in all that time. Neither had he been shingled or shaved, but he rode up to the meetinghouse, tied his horse to the hitching post, and stepped inside. Elder Snow called him to the stand and said to the congregation, 'Here is your new Stake President.' It [was] hard to tell [who] was the most shocked, he or the people. . . .But he accepted the call, and in humility and with fidelity discharged the duties of the office to the best of his ability for 26 years.[9]

NOTES

1. Sherry Pack Baker, "Mormon Media History Timeline, 1827–2007," *BYU Studies,* Volume 47, Number 4, 2009, 121.
2. Ivan J. Barrett, *Heroic Mormon Women* (Covenant Communications, Inc.: American Fork, Utah, 2000), 160–61.
3. boap.org/LDS/Early-Saints/Joel J.-High-on-mount-top.html.
4. Anonymous, "A Venerable Woman: Presendia Lathrop Kimball, Continued," *Woman's Exponent* 12 (October 15, 1883), 75.
5. Oliver R. Smith, ed., *The Journal of Jesse Nathaniel Smith-1834–1906* (Provo: Jesse N. Smith Family Assn., 1970), 274.
6. Lesson Committee, Museum Memories-Daughters of Utah Pioneers (Salt Lake City: Talon Printing, 2010), 2:8.
7. Richard S. Van Wagoner and Steven C. Walker, *A Book of Mormons* (Salt Lake City: Signature Books, 1982), 58.
8. Ibid., 3.
9. International Society Daughters of Utah Pioneers, *Museum Memories* (Salt Lake City, Utah: Talon Printing, 2011), 3: 342–43.

Church Publications

Supplying news to the residents of Utah Territory prior to 1869 was difficult at best, due, mostly in part, from an expensive, inconsistent supply of paper. In an upcoming section you will discover what the Church did to combat this concern. By the turn of the century, with the transcontinental railway well established, commodities such as paper became relatively easier to acquire and less expensive to purchase. However, printing still wasn't cheap. To defray the cost of printing, the Church magazines at that time—*Improvement Era, Juvenile Instructor*, and *Relief Society Magazine*—ran adertisements.[1] You'd be hard press to find advertisements in today's Church publications. However, in the day, it was both common and acceptable.

The newspapers produced by the Church were loaded with articles centered on gospel subjects, the revelations received by the Prophet, experiences of missionaries, the establishment and building of towns the Church occupied, rebuttals of false reports printed in gentile newspapers, and a touch of national and world news. This was the template followed for a number of decades with few articles centered for the youth. For whatever reason, a youth magazine was not on the list of priorities of Church leaders, although as early as 1831 W. W. Phelps was commanded in Doctrine and Covenants 55: "And again, you shall be ordained to assist my servant Oliver Cowdery to do the work of printing, and of selecting and writing books for schools in this church, that little children also may receive instruction before me as is pleasing unto me." What was the catalyst that motivated the eventual publication of youth magazines?

About the time the Church was organized in 1830, fiction, or "cheap printing" as it was termed, became more and more prevalent in American culture. By the 1850s, "dime novels," which obviously had nothing to do with the price of the book since they sold for five cents, became the daily form of entertainment for American families.[2] These novels targeted the youth with sensational plots of crime, romance, and violence, triggering Brigham Young and other Church leaders to speak out against this form of entertainment. They didn't just speak out against the evils of this type of leisure, but provided the youth with alternative choices in wholesome activities along with reading. This was accomplished with the founding of the Young Ladies' Department of the Cooperative Retrenchment Association (which would later be renamed The Young Ladies Mutual Improvement Association) in 1869. Six years later, in 1875, the Young Men's Mutual Improvement Association followed suit. In 1879, the first magazine for the youth, *The Contributor,* was published to wrestle the fiction novels of the day.

Also in the mid-1880s, the Church took additional steps to battle head on the deluge of fiction material provided to young Saints. The completion of the transcontinental railway in 1869 led to the inundation of questionable reading choices for youthful Saints. This was the decade when what was termed "Home Literature" established its way into the homes of the members as a wholesome fictional substitute. Home Literature was written to provide the youth a clean choice for their fictional appetite. The plots were generally based on youth of the Church being given a choice between the Church community and its teachings, or turning their back on their upbringing and their parents' gospel-centered life. In the end, the young man or woman was drawn back into their faith. Susa Young Gates was a strong proponent of the Home Literature movement, writing numerous stories under the pen name "Homespun."[3]

In 1888, Orson F. Whitney stated:

> The formation of a home literature is directly in the line and spirit of this injunction. Literature means learning, and it is from the "best books" we are told to seek it. This does not merely mean the Bible, the Book of Mormon, the book of Doctrine and Covenants, Church works and religious writings—though these indeed are "the best books," and will ever be included in and lie at the very basis of our literature. But it also means history, poetry, philosophy, art and science, languages, government–all truth in fact, wherever found, either local or general, and relating to times past, present or to come.[4]

NOTES

1. Justin R. Bray, "The Lord's Supper During the Progressive Era, 1890–1930, *Journal of Mormon History,* Vol. 38 no. 4, Fall 2012, 99.
2. Michael Harold Paulos, "Smoot Smites Smut": Apostle-Senator Reed

Smoot's 1930 Campaign Against Obscene Books, *Journal of Mormon History,* Fall 2014, 61–62.
3. The 1890s Mormon Culture of Letters and the Post-Manifesto Marriage Crisis, Lisa Olsen Tait, *BYU Studies* Vol. 52, No. 1, 2013, 107–108.
4. Whitney, Orson F. "Home Literature," *The Contributor*, July 1888.

Church Welfare

When I was a boy, my father was hit by a health issue that hospitalized him for about a month. My parents were young and establishing a foothold in life as far as careers were concerned and had just purchased a new home a few years earlier. Money was tight and the timing of my father's health issue added to the stress placed on both my parents. Even though I was too young to understand, I noticed one morning boxes full of food in our hallway. I remember kneeling down beside the boxes and rummaging through them, feeling like it was Christmas morning. I might have asked my mom at the time where the food came from—I don't remember—but today I understand well the purpose of those boxes and how they made it into the hallway of our home.

The Church has always had a vested interest in its members. A sign of this is the food stores they have established throughout the world in what we refer to as bishops' storehouses. This program, where members can donate to help the needy and the sick, has been set in place since the Kirtland years of the Church.

From its inception, when the current Church Welfare Program was announced by President Heber J. Grant as the Church Security Plan during the April 1936 general conference, there has been a number of changes, modifications that no longer exist under the current program.

For instance, under the Security Program, it was possible to donate funds and labor, during the younger and productive stage of an individual's life, that could be drawn out during retirement, or during times of sickness, much the same as the federal government's Social Security program today. It was also possible for those older Saints to earn Church welfare through vicarious work for the dead in the temples.[1]

NOTES

1. Leonard J. Arrington and Wayne K. Hinton, "Origin of the Welfare Plan of The Church of Jesus Christ of Latter-day Saints," *BYU Studies*, Vol. 5, Issue 2, 76.

Customs

The Green and Gold Balls, MIA roadshows, Church basketball, firesides, Church Education Week, Seminary, youth Saturday night dances, the Primary Penny Parade, dance festivals, youth conferences, EFY, Know Your Religion, and many other programs are all part of what used to form or currently form the culture and customs in The Church of Jesus Christ of Latter-day Saints in North America and especially in Utah. All of these things bundled together and glued together with the adhesiveness of our belief as taught in the gospel define who we are as members of The Church of Jesus Christ of Latter-day Saints. It's our imprint.

The pioneers were no different. In fact, much of what the pioneers did has filtered down to us in continuing to hold firm and establish the customs we enjoy in the Church. For instance, one such custom established in the American culture and continued in the early Church on special occasions, at least as early as the Missouri years, was the raising of what was termed Liberty Poles. These poles were especially common during Fourth of July and Pioneer Day festivities. A few of the brethren would look for the tallest tree, cut it down, transport it to wherever the celebration was located, attach a flag (generally a United States flag if one was available, or on some occasions a blanket if there was not a flag to be found), and then raise the pole. One of the first mentions of a Liberty Pole was on July 4, 1838, when on the occasion of the Far West temple cornerstone laying ceremony, Luman A. Shurtiff and others felled a tree, place the United States flag, then raised the pole on the temple site prior to the ceremony.[1]

NOTES

1. Lesson Committee, *Museum Memories* (Salt Lake City: Talon Printing, 2009), 195.

Dancing

Again, similar to the section on Church publications for the youth, this too is one that existed in the early Church and continues today. The "wow" is in the perception of the waltz, also known as the round dance. I recall as a teen, every Saturday night, dances were held at the 17th Avenue stake center in Calgary, Alberta. It was a great time to have fun and socialize with those my age. Much of the dancing was to the favored rock music of the seventies. However, equally fun were the jives, slow dances, and polkas. Little did I realize as a youth the attitude toward dance at the time the Church was first organized and the frowning by leaders on different styles of dance during the Utah Territory years.

Brigham Young believed that the fiddle and dancing were necessary for the recreation of his people and encouraged dancing on both the trail west and once the pioneers settled in the Salt Lake Valley, with him taking the lead in many of the dances. Nonetheless, there was the round dance (the waltz) that so many leaders of the Church struggled with. That was then. We've evolved so that at Church-sponsored dances today, no one is asked to leave for waltzing, or if waltzing is permitted, asked to leave for turning their partner more than twice during the dance.[1] The following two journal entries from Jesse Nathaniel Smith, cousin of the Prophet Joseph Smith, brings to light the attitude of the late nineteenth century:

> November 27, 1881: At Snowflake [Arizona] I gave an account of my recent journey, also of the public teachings of Pres. Taylor and party

> that I heard in Parowan. Spoke upon the evils of dancing. Some did not realize that it was not a part of our religion, while rest and recreation are necessary; believed that as a Church we had lost more than we had gained by dancing, especially had the round dance been termed "the dance of death." Notwithstanding the partial permit of Pres. Taylor I felt to use my influence against round dancing in this stake of Zion.[2]

The following from Jesse N. Smith's journal dated December 18, 1881:

> At a meeting in Snowflake [Arizona] I spoke on the subject of dancing. Reprehended the practice of swinging around in a wanton manner and more times than the figure or the music required. Musicians in the Church who played for round dancing were accessory thereto. Recommended parties to attend dancing schools and learn how to deport themselves properly. Similar remarks were made by Bishops Hunt and Udall and Bro. John A. West.[3]

It's interesting that the round dance did not become popular in the United States until about the mid-nineteenth century. Angus M. Cannon had no problem taking shots during sermons on the evils of the round dance. It was the close embrace and the turning of the couples as they circled around the hall that brought disdain from authorities in the Church. The round dance was never totally axed; it was permitted. However, there were dance rules set, and one of the rules was the number of round dances that could be played in any given evening. This did not just include the number of dances, but extended to the number of times a young man could turn the lady during the dance. The number of round dances was limited from none to three, depending on the ward/bishop, and two was the restricted number of times a lady could be turned on any given round dance.[4] In an official statement issued by the First Presidency in 1912, members were instructed "to avoid dances that require or permit the close embrace."[5]

Bishop Edwin D. Woolley was the one bishop in the Salt Lake City area dead set against round dances in his ward. Simply put, there would be none on his watch. The close embrace of the dancers was enough to work up his ire, but what really broke the camel's back was when the flute player of Olsen's Quadrille Band, the only band in the Salt Lake City area that could play beautifully the "Blue Danube Waltz," showed up to the dance drunk. Bishop Woolley kicked out the band and dismissed any future round dances. To completely dissuade the youth from participating in this form of dance, Edwin Woolley refused to wax the dance floor, stating that he didn't want anyone falling and breaking their necks. This was the mid-1870s when the dance floor was bare planks. To dance the round dance, the couples had to slide their feet, and the bare wood planked floors didn't cut it. They had to be waxed by shaving candles and rubbing into the floor.

It was about this time when Brigham Young challenged all wards to contribute to the St. George Temple building fund. Many of the proceeds from ward dances were being routed to this worthy cause. Bishop Woolley, being of a competitive nature and not wanting to back down from the challenge, met with an enterprising young man in his ward to organize a dance. He explained to the young man his rules. Patiently waiting for the bishop to go through the list of regulations from dance types, to bands, to waxed floors, the young man finally told the bishop he wouldn't make much money. Bishop Woolley couldn't understand why. The young man told him that the young people of Salt Lake City would never come to a dance with such set restrictions. The following conversation then took place:

> Bishop Woolley: "I want you to organize a party. You have more friends among the young people than anyone. I want you to choose your own committee and arrange the whole thing. Make a success of it. We generally lead every other ward in everything we try to do. I want you to be sure to beat them all."
>
> Young man: "I'll do my best, but you'll have to agree to pay the loss if there is one."
>
> BW: (Swallowing hard) "Loss?"
>
> YM: "Yes, you can't have the party in our ward and make any money. The young people won't come any more. In other places they allow them to have three round dances, and you won't have any. I'd rather dance three round dances and throw all the rest away. You've got to have three waltzes."
>
> BW: "All right. Take the three waltzes."
>
> YM: "You won't allow Olsen's Quadrille Band. They're the only people who can play the 'Blue Danube Waltz' well. That draws a crowd. They have the finest cornetist in Salt Lake who will give some cornet solos during the evening."
>
> BW: (Sighing) "Take Olsen's Quadrille Band, take your three round dances, wax your floor!"
>
> YM: "There's something else. You won't allow a Gentile to come. I would like the United States Marshall and one or two high-principled

gentlemen to come and let them see how Mormon boys and girls can behave themselves. There will be no rowdyism. This will be a crowd of the finest kind of young people."

BW: (Defeated) "Invite whom you please."

YM: "I'm going to charge $1.50 instead of $1.00."

BW: "Oh, the people won't pay that!"

YM: "Yes they will, with Olsen's full Quadrille Band."[6]

The young man included Bishop Woolley's son to help head up the dance committee. Tickets of the finest quality were made and then sent to business owners and leaders in the area along with contacts associated with the railroad and ZCMI. Brigham Young's family was also invited. The floor was waxed, posters set on the wall of the General Authorities, and carpets placed in sitting areas.

The night of the dance arrived, and with it Brigham Young and his family. Brigham Young paid ten dollars when answered in the affirmative this dance was to benefit the St. George Temple. During the evening, after the three round dances had played, a fourth waltz was preparing to play in quadrille style. The dancers formed a square like a square dance and danced within the area of the square. Brigham Young noted to the dance organizer that they were waltzing. The dance organizer indicated that they weren't actually waltzing since in a waltz they dance all over the floor, but rather this was a quadrille. Brigham Young laughed as he stated, "Oh, you boys, you boys."

The dance was a success. Bishop Edwin Woolley was happy to present Brigham Young with eighty dollars from the profits of the dance, which happened to be far more than any other ward. Who was the young man that organized the dance? None other than Heber J. Grant.[7]

So yes, we continue to dance today just as the pioneer Saints did. This really is not much of a change. However, I'm sure you understand there was a shift in attitude, the way we view the waltz today, compared to the Church leaders' view at the time of Brigham Young.

NOTES

1. Oliver R. Smith, ed., *The Journal of Jesse Nathaniel Smith-1834–1906* (Provo: Jesse N. Smith Family Assn., 1970), 259.
2. Ibid., 257–58.
3. Ibid., 259.

4. Donald Q. Cannon and David J. Whittaker, *Supporting Saints: Life Stories of Nineteenth-Century Mormons* (Salt Lake City: Bookcraft Inc., 1985), 379.
5. Ibid., 379.
6. Heber J. Grant, "Gospel Standards" (Salt Lake City: *Improvement Era* Publication: 1943), 280–82; as found in Judy Fraser, *Hidden Treasures from Church History* (Orem, Utah: Granite Publishing and Distribution, 1996), 155–58.
7. Ibid.

Death Bed Rituals

This practice concerned those dying who asked for a blessing. Those who felt like life was at an end, and knew death was imminent, were then anointed, blessed, and dedicated to God. This continues today when priesthood holders offer blessings to those about to depart this sphere. It appears that women also offered this for women in the early Church. The following is from Caroline Crosby in 1846: "I went to visit her, washed and anointed her from head to foot, with sister P's help." She continues, "She seemed very anxious to live to receive her endowments in the temple and we also felt very sorry that she could not. I anointing her, inadvertently told her, that it was for her burial. Notwithstanding my anxiety to have her live. But the words some way pressed themselves out of my mouth."[1]

When called on a mission to Britain, missionary Samuel W. Richards and other elders visited a member of the Church in New York City prior to sailing to England. A Sister Lincoln was ill and fading. The elders administered the sacrament for her, then anointed her with oil and blessed her unto the day of her burial by the laying on of hands.[2]

In 1865, Wilford Woodruff recorded the following: "Called upon Sister Gray who had a canser in the breast which was Eating her Vitals and rotting her flesh. President Young, Cannon, & myself laid hands upon her. She wished us to pray that she might speedily die as she

Could not live. President Young dedicated her to God for her death & burial. In about 12 hours she died."[3]

Finally, Sister Susan Julia Martineau professed: "She was satisfied with life, and desired to go." She lacked the desire to live as a result of a long and painful sickness. She "wished me [James Martineau] to bring the elders, and give her up, provided she could not be healed. J.E. Hyde came in, and he and I dedicated her to the Lord and gave her up—to His will. It was a hard thing for a husband to do—oh, so hard."[4]

In the October 1922 *Improvement Era,* Heber J. Grant, Charles W. Penrose, and Anthony W. Ivins of the First Presidency instructed:

> The custom which is growing in the Church to dedicate those who appear to be beyond recovery, to the Lord, has no place among the ordinances of the Church. The Lord has instructed us, where people are sick, to call in the elders, two or more, who should pray for and lay their hands upon them in the name of the Lord; and "If they die," says the Lord, "they shall die unto me; and if they live, they shall live unto me." No possible advantage can result from dedicating faithful members of the Church to the Lord prior to their death. Their membership in the Church, their devotion to the faith which they have espoused, are sufficient guarantee, so far as their future welfare is concerned.
>
> The administration of the ordinances of the Gospel to the sick, is for the purpose of healing them, that they may continue lives of usefulness until the Lord shall call them hence. This is as far as we should go. If we adhere strictly to that which the Lord has revealed in regard to this matter, no mistake will be made.[5]

NOTES

1. Edward Leo Lyman, Susan Ward Payne, and S. George Ellsworth, eds., *No Place to Call Home: The 1807–1857 Life Writings of Caroline Barnes Crosby, Chronicler of Outlying Mormon Communities* (Logan: Utah State University Press, 2005), 64–65.
2. Samuel W. Richards, Diary, September 11, 1846, microfilm of holograph, L. Tom Perry Special Collections, Harold B. Lee Library, Brigham Young University.
3. Wilford Woodruff, *Wilford Woodruff's Journal, 1833–1898, Typescript,* ed. Scott G. Kenney, 9 vols. (Midvale, Utah: Signature Books, 1983–84), 3:441.
4. Donald G. Godfrey and Rebecca S. Martineau-McCarty, eds., *Uncommon Common Pioneer, The Journals of James Henry Martineau,*

1828–1918 (Provo, Utah: Religious Studies Center, Brigham Young University, 2008), 174.

5. First Presidency, "On Dedication the Sick and the Suffering to the Lord," *Improvement Era 25* (October 1922): 1122.

Disfellowships/ Excommunications

What was done in one ward or stake, or by one bishop or stake president in the early years, may not necessarily translate the same throughout the Church. I believe much of the same situation exists in today's Church. There are those leaders who administer the letter of the law in their wards or stakes, as opposed to others who govern by the spirit of the law. I remember years ago a good friend telling me the plight his wife faced in their ward. She believed that the only meeting she was required to attend was sacrament meeting. The bishop refused to give her a temple recommend, pointing out the fact that she was not making an effort to attend all of her meetings. His wife continued to attend sacrament meeting only and refused callings when given the opportunity. Soon the ward boundaries were realigned. The realignment found my friend in a new ward. He shared with me that it was just a matter of time before the new bishop called his wife into his office. The bishop told her that he noticed she didn't have a temple recommend and asked if she didn't mind sharing with him why. His wife explained her lack of meeting attendance and because of this was refused a recommend. The bishop surprised her when he stated that this isn't the way he operated in this ward and proceeded to give her a recommend, no strings attached. What's interesting, within a few months, his wife was attending all of her meetings and immersed in a calling.

The following from the journal of Jesse N. Smith dated June 6, 1862, is a prime example: "Mrs. Karen Thomsen presented me a bottle of wine, and requested me to baptize her, which I did at 10 p.m. She and her husband had formerly belonged to the Church, but had been cut off for not paying their tithing."[1]

This wouldn't exist today. No one would be disfellowshipped for non-payment of tithes. About the worst case scenario today is your temple recommend may not be re-issued depending on the circumstance.

How about refusal to serve a mission after called? "In June, 1833 . . . the Bishop's Council, and a Council of twelve High Priests, was organized. . . . It was at the same Council that Daniel Copley, a timid young man, who had been ordained a Priest, and required to go and preach the Gospel, was called to an account for not going on his mission. The young man said he was too weak to attempt to preach, and the Council cut him off the Church. I wonder what our missionaries now would think of so rigid a discipline as was given at that time thirty one years ago, under the immediate supervision of the Prophet."[2]

The following from *The Joseph Smith Papers*: "June 21, 1833: The President's Court, also took brother Daniel Copley's Priest's Licence and Membership from him, because he refused to fulfil his mission according to the council of the High Priesthood of the holy order of God" [HC 1:354].[3]

In Britain it was not unusual to cut off members from the Church for moral sins, which can be the case today. However, it sometimes ran far deeper than this. For instance, if the offender did not have an attitude of remorse, it was typical to be cut off from the Church for such things as lying, swearing, or missing meetings without a cause.[3] With time (1840s and 1850s) Church leaders in England realized that maybe the elders and branch presidents were being a little too stringent and suggested not to cut off or withdraw membership for not attending meetings.[4]

Joseph F. Merrill tells of a meeting when Bishop Marvin O. Ashton shared the following two stories related to those leaders who administer by the spirit of the law as opposed to those who govern by the letter of the law. In the first instance, certain boys in a ward created some Halloween mischief. The bishop invited the pranksters to come to sacrament meeting and offer a public apology for their mischief on pains of excommunication if they so refused. Today, some of these boys have grown to men and are no longer part of the ward family, but rather raising families outside of the Church. In the second story Bishop Ashton told of a wedding party held at his home. Refreshments were called for. However, it was discovered the ice box housing the said refreshments was empty. The bishop determined the culprits. Another social was organized, and this time twice the amount of ice cream was provided for refreshments. The boys were invited to the social. As the young men waited to be served, one young lad started crying. This created a chain reaction, and soon all the boys involved were crying. The kind actions of the second bishop led to young men that grew up in the Church, becoming some of the strongest leaders in the area.[5]

Author Leon Harthshorn wrote:

> The two bishops of the story were undoubtedly actuated by the best of motives. Not for a moment would I question that. But one bishop was wise and the other unwise. The thought in the mind of one was to use persuasion, long-suffering, gentleness, meekness, and love, so beautifully stated in the revelation noted. In the case of the other bishop he seems to have acted impulsively. He forgot the scriptural injunction found in Doctrine and Covenants 64:9–10: "Wherefore, I say unto you, that ye ought to forgive one another; for he that forgiveth not his brother his trespasses standeth condemned before the Lord; for there remaineth in him the greater sin. I, the Lord, will forgive whom I will forgive, but of you it is required to forgive all men."[6]

NOTES

1. Oliver R. Smith, ed., *The Journal of Jesse Nathaniel Smith—1834–1906* (Provo: Jesse N. Smith Family Assn., 1970), 76.
2. *Journal of Discourses,* Tuesday, November 15, 1864, 11:8; see also josephsmithpapers.org/paper-summary/minutes-21–june-1833/2
3. Minutes, 21 June 1833, josephsmithpapers.org.
4. Rebecca Bartholomew, *Audacious Women-Early British Mormon Immigrants* (Salt Lake City: Signature Books, 1995), 48.
5. Rebecca Bartholomew, *Audacious Women-Early British Mormon Immigrants*, 96.
6. Leon R. Hartshorn, *Exceptional Stories from the Lives of Early Apostles* (Provo, Utah: Spring Creek Book Company, 2004), 104–105.

Donations

Sarah M. Kimball resided in Nauvoo when the walls of the temple rose three feet over the foundation. It was about this time when Sarah and her husband's son was born (November 22, 1841). The Kimballs were people of means. Understanding this, Sarah wished to donate to the construction of the temple. There was an issue, though. Sarah was a member, but her affluent husband was not. One day, as Sarah laid in bed with their newborn son, Mr. Kimball came over, sitting on the bed and admiring the baby, when Sarah initiated the following conversation.

> "What is the boy worth?" He replied, "O, I don't know, he is worth a great deal." I said, "Is he worth a thousand dollars?" Mr. Kimball replied, "Yes, more than that if he lives and does well." "Then I have something to help on the Temple." Continuing, Sarah stated, "Half of him is mine, is it not?" "Yes, I suppose so." "Then I have something to help on the Temple." "You have?" he inquired. "Yes, and I think of turning my share right in as tithing." Mr. Kimball realized she had him, and closed the conversation with, "Well, I'll have to see about that."[1]

It wasn't long before Sarah's husband bumped into Joseph Smith. Now was as good a time as any to explain the dilemma he was in. Joseph listened. After understanding the facts, the Prophet presented two options: 1) keep the child and give $500 to the Church, or 2) give the child to the Church and receive $500. Since Mr. Kimball possessed a large amount of property in the Nauvoo area, he chose option number 1 by deeding property just north of the temple.[1]

It's interesting the fund-making concepts the Saints brainstormed as a way to further the construction of temples. During the Utah years of the Church when the St. George, Manti, Logan, and Salt Lake temples were being constructed, the sisters determined to donate to the cause from the sale of eggs laid by their chickens on Sunday. These eggs were christened "Sunday eggs."[2]

Whether eggs or direct cash donations, as in the next story, the results were basically the same. The donation benefited both the Church and the Saints providing the funds. In the case of the eggs, the Church was able to provide a temple. This temple benefitted the Saints as a result of the blessings derived from serving in the house of the Lord. The same is true of

O. C. Beebe and his generous cash donation. As a member of the General Board of Y.M.M.I.A from 1905–12, O. C. Beebe donated $600 to the South African mission. Why he donated to this mission, I don't know. What I do know is the donation didn't go unnoticed. The Church felt he was deserving of a reward because of his generosity. As a result, Brother Beebe was credited with having served a two-year mission.[3]

Donations to the construction of temples was a way of life for the Saints. Those belonging to the Church were an impoverished people. Nevertheless, they were able time and time again to give in small ways to the construction, not only to the Kirtland and Nauvoo temples, but also the four pioneer temples built in Utah Territory. Benjamin F. Johnson reminisced in his autobiography about a meeting prior to the dedication of the Kirtland Temple. This was a blessing meeting for those who had donated their labor toward the construction of the Lord's house. Benjamin enjoyed the meeting and prayed inwardly that there would be a blessing in store for him under the hands of the Prophet of God, Joseph Smith. How could this be, though, he questioned himself. He had not physically worked on the temple, but yet the hope was vibrant in his soul. As the last blessing was given, Joseph Smith asked his brother Hyrum if there was not one more deserving of a blessing. Hyrum walked through the congregation, finally coming side to side with Benjamin, who was standing by the door. Hyrum asked Brother Johnson if he had labored on the temple. Benjamin's hope seemed to fade as the only right answer was that he hadn't. Hyrum then asked if he had donated to help the building of the temple. Yes, he had. Benjamin donated a new rifle and helped make brick that was used during the construction of the temple. Benjamin's dream was realized as Hyrum escorted him to the front of the room, where, under the hands of a Prophet of God, he received the much sought after blessing.[4]

Years ago, while employed by the Alberta Forest Service, I happened to be stationed in the small village of Wandering River. Yes, the place was as small as its name. The only church in the area was an Anglican church. I developed a friendship with one of the families in town. We became good friends and had numerous religious discussions. I'd never had anyone request a Book of Mormon, Doctrine and Covenants, Pearl of Great Price and all three volumes of *Doctrines of Salvation*, as this couple did. I attended services with him at the Anglican church. This was the second time in my life when I've experienced the plate passed throughout the congregation for the purpose of collecting money. It didn't come as a shock to my system to see the plate passed aisle by aisle through the chapel. I understood the purpose of the donations. Believe it or not, this also occurred in The Church of Jesus Christ of Latter-day Saints during the 1839 mission to Britain. A plate was passed during meetings with the money funneled to the poor and the support of the missionaries. This practice wasn't confined to sacrament type meetings only. The missionaries, as they preached in rented halls, also passed a collection plate to cover the cost of rent.[5] Today, this practice no longer exists in the Church. It doesn't need to. Outside all clerk offices in all Church buildings are donation slips and envelopes that allow the Saints to donate to whatever cause they so desire. One aspect that has never changed throughout Church history is the members have always been a generous and a donating people.

NOTES

1. mormonwomenhistory.org/final/biographies/smk.html
2. Richard E. Bennett, "Which is the Wisest Course," The Transformation in Mormon Temple Consciousness, 1870–1898, *BYU Studies* Vol. 52, No. 2, 2013, 28–29.
3. Andrew Jenson, *L.D.S. Biographical Encyclopedia* (Salt Lake City: Andrew Jensen Memorial Association, 1936), 4:231–32.
4. Benjamin F. Johnson, *My Life's Review* (Independence, Missouri: Zion's Printing and Publishing Co., 1947), 7–107.
5. James B. Allen et. al, *Men With a Mission 1837–1841* (Salt Lake City: Deseret Book, 1992), 102–103.

Education

The following from the *Times and Seasons,* as found in *The Joseph Smith Papers*, gives an indication of the seriousness with which the Saints viewed education during the Nauvoo years of the Church:

> The "University of the City of Nauvoo," will enable us to teach our children wisdom—to instruct them in all knowledge, and learning, in

> the Arts, Sciences and Learned Professions. We hope to make this institution one of the great lights of the world, and by and through it, to diffuse that kind of knowledge which will be of practical utility, and for the public good, and also for private and individual happiness. The Regents of the University[24] will take the general supervision of all mat[t]ers appertaining to education from common schools up to the highest branches of a most liberal collegiate course. They will establish a regular system of education, and hand over the pupil from teacher to professor, until the regular gradation is consummated, and the education finished.[1]

However, this didn't stop at Nauvoo, or pre-Nauvoo for this fact, but would eventually carry to the Salt Lake Valley. Education in Utah is a fascinating study. The Saints were seeking obscurity when they turned their backs on the United States and located themselves in the western desert. High on the list of priorities, when they first entered the Salt Lake Valley, was the establishment of schools. It was not uncommon for children to attend school in tents, covered wagons, in log structures, or under open skies. The pioneers envisioned total obscurity, and for a time relished the seclusion. Little did the leaders of The Church of Jesus Christ of Latter-day Saints and their followers understand the changing tide soon to engulf them with the arrival of the California Gold Rush seekers in 1849 and Johnston's army in 1858. The federal occupation of Utah during the Civil War brought another army, resulting in the discovery of silver in 1863, which led to another influx of outsiders. Finally, the transcontinental railroad in 1869 dealt the fatal blow to the solitude. Ironically, because of a strong outside presence, Presbyterian schools began to dot the landscape. With time these schools vied for and, in many cases, experienced success among the Saints when the pioneers sent their children to these schools. Between 1869 to 1890, ninety such schools were established in Utah with a student population of 7,000, half of which were members of the Church.[2]

Alarmed at the growing trend, the Church confronted the situation with the establishment of stake academies. From 1875 to 1910, The Church of Jesus Christ of Latter-day Saints operated thirty-three stake academies, many of which no longer exist today. It's interesting that a few still exist in the form of current universities and colleges. For instance, St. Joseph Stake Academy is currently Eastern Arizona College, and those attending Brigham Young University would have been students in Brigham Young Academy. The Salt Lake Stake Academy now graces the name of Ensign College. Those living in the Ogden area were most likely educated in the Weber Stake Academy, which is now Weber State University. Snow College in Ephraim, Utah, back in the day, schooled students under the name of Sanpete Stake Academy. Not too many years ago, Brigham Young University–Idaho was Ricks College, and previous to this, Bannock Stake Academy. And finally, St. George Stake Academy later became Dixie State College.[3]

In addition to stake academies, Joseph F. Smith recognized the need to establish an afterschool program for those too young to attend academies. When the Saints first entered the valley, it was not uncommon for the Bible and Book of Mormon to be used as texts for children's education. As the federal government gained greater control in Utah Territory, with time, it forced the stop of spiritual related material in the classroom. The idea of the afterschool class, which became known as the religion class, was to teach children both secular and spiritual related courses, minus the government interference.[4] Like the Primary, the religion class met one afternoon a week in a meetinghouse. This class operated from 1890 to the time it was dissolved in 1929, at which time it was absorbed into the Primary Association.[5]

Ward schools for children also became popular. In fact, most wards had schools.

Adult education was viewed just as important as that of children. It was important enough that the Prophet Joseph Smith organized the first adult education school in America when he established the School of the Prophets. This was formed in Kirtland, but what some might not realize is this school sporadically continued, even after the Saints arrived in the Rocky Mountains.

Ida Cook, in 1885, along with the Logan Temple Association, organized an adult education class that was conducted in the Logan temple once monthly. This hour-long class instructed the students in theology, philosophy, civil government, domestic and political economy, languages, and history.[6]

NOTES

1. josephsmithpapers.org/paper-summary/proclamation-15–january-1841/3
2. Val Brinkerhoff, "The Symbolism of the Beehive in Latter-day Saint Tradition," *BYU Studies* Vol. 52, No. 2, 2013, 47.

3. Arnold K. Garr, Donald Q. Cannon, and Richard O. Cowan, *Encyclopedia of Latter-day Saint History* (Salt Lake City: Deseret Book, 2000), 4–5.
4. The Symbolism of the Beehive in Latter-day Saint Tradition, Val Brinkerhoff, *BYU Studies* Vol. 52, No. 2, 2013, 49–50.
5. Richard O. Cowan, *The Latter-day Saint Century* (Salt Lake City: Bookcraft, 1999), 106–7; Andrew Jensen, *Encyclopedic History of The Church of Jesus Christ of Latter-day Saints* (Salt Lake City: Deseret News, 1941), 697.
6. Vicky Burgess-Olsen, *Sister Saints* (Vicky Burgess-Olsen: 1978), 254.

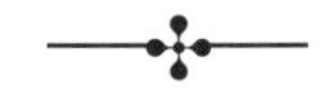

Endowment House Requirements

The Saints would fail to enjoy a house dedicated to the Lord in which to perform both ordinances for the living and the dead for over three decades. Understanding the need, Brigham Young remedied the situation when he called for the construction of the Endowment House on the northwest corner of the temple block in Salt Lake City in 1854; it was completed in 1855. The inspiration behind the decision came from a revelation given to the Prophet Joseph Smith as found in Doctrine and Covenants 124:29–30, which states, "For a baptismal font there is not upon the earth that they, my saints, may be baptized for those who are dead—For this ordinance belongeth to my house, and cannot be acceptable to me, only in the days of your poverty, wherein ye are not able to build a house unto me."[1]

When the Endowment House initially opened in 1855, and continuing through the first year after its dedication, worthiness was expected, but there failed to exist an interview process that would solidify the merit of the candidate. In 1856, President Heber C. Kimball advised the following questions be asked prior to those interested in attending the Endowment House:

- Pay tithing from year to year.
- Pray in your families.
- Do not speak against the authorities of the Church and kingdom of God.
- Do not steal.
- Do not lie.
- Do not swear.
- Do not interfere with the neighbors' things or spouses.
- Respect presiding officers and the bishop.[1]

NOTES

1. Ronald W. Walker and Doris R. Dant ed., *Nearly Everything Imaginable* (Provo, Utah: BYU Press, 1999), 275.

Endowments

During the Nauvoo years, endowments were first performed in Joseph Smith's red brick store. For example, on May 28, 1843, Joseph and Emma Smith were married for time and eternity in the store.[1] Endowments outside of the temple continued once the Saints were settled in the Salt Lake Valley. Prior to 1850, Louisa Barnes Pratt stated that she very much wanted her husband, Addison Pratt, to receive his endowment. At this point, Utah Territory lacked a temple. The Council House was yet to be constructed (1852), in which endowments took place until the Endowment House was built in 1855. The only locations where the Saints could receive their endowment in Utah Territory, prior to 1852, was in the home of Brigham Young, or in the case of Addison, on the top of Ensign Peak.[2] For those who might struggle with temple ordinances being performed outside the walls of these holy edifices, John Taylor provides relief: "Although it is very important that Temples should be built, the Priesthood is not for the Temple, but the Temples are for the priesthood, and while the Saints are doing all in their power to build Temples, the Lord will accept our ordinances performed, under [certain] conditions, in a place, if it is not a regular temple, that has been especially set apart for these purposes."[3]

Apparently, there was a time during the Nauvoo years of the Church when, similar to baptisms and patriarchal blessings, one could be washed and anointed on more than one occasion. Lucy White Flake said, "As we wished to go and work in the Temple and it was council for all to get baptized before going. . . . I was adopted to my Father and Mother. . . . This labor was a great comfort to us. . . . We received our second Washings and anointing. They said as we were coming a way so far we could receive them but they never had given them to any one so young. . . . We were in Heaven sure when we were working in that Holy place but when we get out Stan doubles his force on a person trying to make up for the good one receives."[4]

NOTES

1. kosephsmithpapers.org
2. Vicky Burgess-Olsen, *Sister Saints* (Vicky Burgess-Olsen: 1978), 47–48.
3. Richard E. Bennett, "Which is the Wisest Course," The Transformation in Mormon Temple Consciousness, 1870–1898, *BYU Studies* Vol. 52, No. 2, 2013, 10.
4. Leonard J. Arrington and David Bitton, *Saints Without Halos* (Salt Lake City: Signature Books, 1982), 73, 77.

Funerals

During my junior high days, my best friend was a man in his seventies. I enjoyed walking to his home, where he taught me how to grind, shape, and polish stones into tie pins and a necklace. He was patient and kind and always fun to be around. I remember coming home from Scouts one evening when my parents broke the sad news to me that he had passed away. My parents and I attended his funeral, the first one I had experienced in my young life. When we went into the Relief Society room, there, surrounded by family, was the body of my best friend as he lay in his casket. I can't remember, but I'm sure my parents, understanding that I had never experienced a funeral before, educated me on what to expect. I'm certain they asked me if I wanted to view my friend laying in his casket. Having experienced this, I assumed this is the way we have always conducted funerals in the Church, and was somewhat amazed to learn that this isn't the case.

In the preface of this book I state that many of the changes in the material presented were Church-wide practices, or in some cases the practices could be at a stake or ward level conditional on the feelings or beliefs of local leaders. It's possible that funerals were one such practice. We know that the Saints viewed the bodies of Joseph and Hyrum Smith in the Mansion House in Nauvoo after their martyrdom. Nevertheless, at the funeral of Abraham H. Cannon, Church authorities discouraged the custom of viewing the body: "It is needless to say to intelligent Latter-day Saints that all this is repugnant to that spirit and decorum which ought to characterize the laying away of the earthly tabernacles of those whom we have loved or respected; and the general authorities of the Church have felt called upon to exert an influence to check this evil, and have advised the Saints not to expose their dead to public view."[1]

The Saints in Snowflake, Arizona, had an interesting local practice of leaving the coffin at home while the community attended the funeral. Lucy [Flake] asked Elder Francis M. Lyman if what the community was doing was correct. She "asked him if it was right for our dead to be left at home while the friends went to the meeting house. . . . He seemed very much out of patiance. . . . He said no, take them to the meeting house every time."[2]

NOTES

1. Richard S. Van Wagoner and Steven C. Walker, *A Book of Mormons* (Salt Lake City; Signature Books, 1982), 43.
2. David F. Boone, "As Bad As I Hated To Come," Lucy Hannah White Flake in Arizona, *Journal of Mormon History,* Vol. 38, No. 4, Fall 2012, 76.

Gathering to Zion

Again, I'm stepping from the scope of this book and not sharing anything new when I share a little about the Church's migration efforts from Europe to the United States, continuing through to Winter Quarters and finally, the Salt Lake Valley. I mentioned in the preface that I desired to share change in the Church coupled with a "wow" factor. This hardly qualifies. In fact, I'm certain many who read this book can trace their family histories to ancestors who braved the Atlantic crossing, only to continue on the trail west to Utah Territory. It's obvious we don't practice this today. Zion is now defined as where the Saints dwell. I'm sure all of us have heard the General Authorities speak during conference and state that the gathering for the Japanese is in Japan, for the Russians in Russia, and for the Brazilians in Brazil. There's absolutely no "wow" factor in this. What makes it worse, you didn't learn a thing. The only reason I feel it important enough to include is because of the amount of money that was expended by the combined effort of the Church and through individual donations. I was shocked when I read in *BYU Studies* that approximately $10 million was spent in the effort to bring 80,000 people to this valley, which definitely spells wow![1]

NOTE

1. Leonard J. Arrington, Religion and Economics in Mormon History, *BYU Studies,* Vol. 3 No. 3, 1961, 21–22.

Genealogy

During the early years of Salt Lake City, since there was very little money, people often traded services or used produce as a medium of exchange. I once read of a young man on a date using a turkey to pay for him and his date to enter the theater in Salt Lake City. The turkey was worth more than the price of admission, and the man received in "change" two chickens that he and his date held throughout the duration of the date. This practice survived for many years. However, with the increase of available money and industry, money became the mode of exchange for services, food, clothing, and household items. During the Great Depression of the 1930s the practice of using produce to pay for services resumed on occasion in the Salt Lake Valley. It was during this time that bishops permitted the "worthy" poor to pay for genealogical research by Church researchers using produce.[1]

The 1930s saw other change introduce regarding genealogy. In 1932, Monday evening became the chosen evening for genealogical classes. The transition wasn't smooth in all stakes. For instance, in 1936 one stake president felt it imperative to designate Monday evening as "home night." Joseph Fielding Smith sent the following in a letter to this stake president:

> It was reported that in your stake there was a move on foot to make Monday evening "Home Night," thus taking away from the genealogical workers the night on which they meet.
>
> Elder Joseph Fielding Smith suggested that Saturday evening be termed "Home night," as a way to "put a stop to Saturday night parties and dances, which interfere so materially with the Sunday Schools the following morning."[2]

Also of interest, the fourth Monday evening of each month was genealogical home teaching week, where those in the genealogical class visited their home teaching families, sharing with them helpful tips in genealogical research. The fifth Sunday of each month was also declared "genealogical Sunday." Sacrament meeting was devoted to talks from the pulpit centered around family history.[3]

During the late 1920s, bishops became concerned at the lack of temple attendance. As a way to accelerate temple attendance, bishops labored with ward genealogical committees by calling people on temple missions. These missions were generally given to the elderly and unemployed for a duration of three months. The expectation for attendance was one day in a week. In 1934 Elder Joseph Fielding Smith opposed these calls, stating this was a member's responsibility anyway. He felt the practice was no different than calling people on missions to attend sacrament meeting. Elder Smith's thoughts were protested by some fearing that axing these missions would leave the temples virtually empty. In 1935, temple attendance mission calls were no longer issued. However, it was said that some stakes resurrected the calls for a short time in 1949.[4]

In Primary the children sing, "I love to see the temple. I'm going there someday.[5] Today, the best a Primary-aged child can hope for is to view the temple. But there was a time when the Primary Association was instrumental in the work for the dead. As early as 1922 and into 1923, Primary children ages eight to twelve years of age entered the temple and performed nearly 50,000 proxy baptisms.[6]

Also during the 1930s, the book of remembrance project received its beginnings. In October 1930, Elder Joseph Fielding Smith created twelve genealogical lessons for the youth, ages twelve to twenty-one, to enhance their family history skills. This snowballed into the creation of the book of remembrances. I imagine many are familiar with and hold in their possession today these books devoted to their personal genealogy and family history. However, with time they have slowly phased out into near extinction.

I remember during the 1970s, my parents purchased for me and each one of my siblings a book of remembrance. They were about 8.5x14 inches in size. The reason for the odd-ball form was to fit pedigree charts and family group sheets configured in this form. The design was standard. However, color and choice of temple engraved on the cover were according to personal taste. Since my parents were married in the Idaho Falls Temple, this was a natural option to grace the top cover of my mother's book of remembrance. Mine? There were sixteen temples throughout the world at the time. It was a tough decision, so I had all sixteen temples emblazoned on the cover encircling the words "Book of Remembrance." Along with group sheets and pedigree charts, my Aaronic Priesthood and MIA advancement certificates, in addition to awards received in Scouts, and school were displayed in the book. These weren't binder style but rather had a locking mechanism on the side that held all the sheets in place. A person could thicken their book by screwing in metal extension pegs. I remember my mother's book was thick and heavy. Technology is slowly squeezing the life from and making the books of remembrance a thing of the past. Out of curiosity, I googled "LDS book of remembrance" and discovered that they can be purchased online. I was shocked when I discovered that the family group sheets and pedigree charts can also be ordered. My guess is that with time—and not very much time, most likely when my generation dies out—books of remembrance will no longer exist.[7]

During the 1950s, additional concerns were created all in the name of genealogy, leading to practices that no longer exists. For instance, because women generally attend the temple in larger numbers than men, there was a scarcity of female names. To combat this, the Logan Temple district held special priesthood sessions on George Washington's birthday. In 1953, stake presidents in the Logan Temple district, instructed by the president of the Logan Temple, directed that women were expected to bring their own family name to the temple. There simply wasn't enough female names to give to those sisters attending the temple; the supply was completely exhausted.[8] In fact, the issue of providing names to the temple by the genealogical society was in crisis mode during the early 1960s. Try as the Church might, the leaders were unsuccessful at persuading members to research their families to find names to take to the temples. In 1958, temple attendance was up 29 percent from the previous year. However, the lack of names led to cutbacks in the number of temple sessions. By 1960, the situation became so dire that the genealogical society workers were working overtime, night shifts, and holidays to keep a steady stream of names, even going so far as to run names to the Salt Lake Temple each day just to keep it open.[9]

Then the miracle came. In 1976, Alex Haley's book *Roots* was released. Since then, providing names to the temples has become a non-issue. Home computers, with the associated genealogical software, serve as another modern-day miracle.

NOTES

1. Genealogical Society Minutes, 22 March 1929, in James B. Allen, Jessie L. Embry, Kahlile B. Mehr, *Hearts Turned to the Fathers* (Provo, Utah: BYU Studies, 1995), 109.
2. James B. Allen, Jessie L. Embry, Kahlile B. Mehr, *Hearts Turned to the Fathers*, 117–118.
3. Ibid.
4. Ibid., 188.
5. *Children's Songbook*, The Church of Jesus Christ of Latter-day Saints, 1989, 95.
6. Clara W. Beebe, "Temple Work," *Children's Friend* 23 (November 1924): 342 in James B. Allen, Jessie L. Embry, Kahlile B. Mehr, *Hearts Turned to the Father*, 119.

7. James B. Allen, Jessie L. Embry, Kahlile B. Mehr, *Hearts Turned to the Fathers*, 119.
8. A. George Raymond President of the Logan Temple, to all stake presidents, 15 April 1953, genealogical correspondence in James B. Allen, Jessie L. Embry, Kahlile B. Mehr, *Hearts Turned to the Fathers*, 175.
9. James B. Allen, Jessie L. Embry, Kahlile B. Mehr, *Hearts Turned to the Fathers*, 176.

General Authorities

In February 1835, in Kirtland, the Three Witnesses selected twelve men to form the Quorum of the Twelve. Their roll and authority at the time in no way replicates what the Quorum of the Twelve does at present. In a sense, the 1835 quorum were a traveling high council away from the Church center (Kirtland). When in Kirtland, these men did not hold local authority. With time, over the years, Joseph Smith would add to their authority. In fact, at a Nauvoo August 1841 conference, Joseph Smith shocked those in attendance when he assigned Brigham Young the responsibility to preside. Why the shock? Because the Quorum of the Twelve were not permitted to lead meetings other than outside of Church headquarters.[1]

But the way things were done back then as opposed to now didn't end. The history of those called to serve as General Authorities is replete with modifications from previous decades to the way the current Church position is viewed today. For instance, John Willard Young, on February 4, 1864, was ordained the youngest apostles at nineteen years of age.[2] Even though John Willard Young never served in the Quorum of the Twelve, he honored this sacred appointment under the hands of his prophet-father, Brigham Young, by serving over the Salt Lake Stake, as a missionary to England, and as a counselor to his father.[3]

Wilford Woodruff shares additional information on this situation:

> President Young said, "I am going to tell you something that I have never before mentioned to any other person. I have ordained my sons,

> Joseph A., Brigham & John W., Apostles and My Counselors. Have you any objections?' J. Taylor and G. A. Smith said they had not, that it was his own affair & they considered it under his own direction. He further stated, 'In ordaining my sons I have done no more than I am perfectly willing that you should do with yours. And I am determined to put my sons into active service in the Spiritual Affairs of the kingdom and keep them there just as long as possible. You have the same privilege.'"[4]

Another instance occurred in April 1880 when the Council of the Seventy met to determine who should fill the vacancy created by the death of Elder Albert P. Rockwood. As it was, those involved in this discussion experienced difficulty aligning on who should be accorded this honor. President Joseph Young favored William Whittaker Taylor, son of President John Taylor, as the new recipient. Finally, after continued discussion with little headway, President Joseph Young suggested that those names being considered should be written on a separate slip of paper. After this task was completed and the names were placed in a box, President Joseph Young turned his back to the box and instructed Seymour B. Young to pull one slip from the box at a time and to inform Joseph when the slip was pulled, but not to divulge the name. Elder Joseph Young indicated that when the slip of paper with the name of the individual worthy to fill this position was pulled, the Spirit would whisper to him to have the name read. The first slip was pulled. Elder Young's response was, "Go on." The same response was given when the second slip was pulled. Nevertheless, when the third slip of paper was pulled, Joseph Young asked for the name to be read. The name? William Whittaker Taylor.[5]

It's our current procedure in The Church of Jesus Christ of Latter-day Saints to sustain all General Authorities in general conference. However, this hasn't always been the case. In 1842, Orson Pratt was excommunicated from the Church. To fill the vacancy created in the Quorum of the Twelve Apostles, Amasa Lyman was called by Brigham Young. It was a matter of months later when Orson Pratt repented, was re-baptized, and reinstated as an apostle. This created a new issue, an obvious fact that there were now thirteen men in the Quorum of the Twelve. The issue was resolved with the reassignment of Amasa Lyman as a counselor in the First Presidency. Elder Lyman was never sustained as an apostle in a general conference or a counselor during Brigham Young's lifetime.[6]

Other oddities surrounding ordinations to the apostleship include the incident surrounding Joseph F. Smith on July 1, 1866. On this day Brigham Young secretly ordained Joseph F. Smith to be an apostle and one of his counselors in the First Presidency. Not even Brigham Young's current first counselor knew of the ordination. It's interesting that Joseph F. Smith served for thirty-eight years in the First Presidency as counselor to Brigham Young, John Taylor, Wilford Woodruff, and Lorenzo Snow.[7]

Today we live in an age of communication like never before. With the emergence of cell phones we can now communicate with each other immediately. I'm not sharing anything new when I state it hasn't always been this way. Just in my lifetime there have been massive advancements in technology. When I was a kid, we had dial phones (push button phones hadn't arrived on the scene; beside a push button phone would seem far too spaced-aged), and we absolutely had no idea what a video store was. Renting movies was still something in the far out future. The norm was two TV channels, with me acting as my dad's remote. So, understanding this, how did the early Church, during the Kirtland years, inform an individual they would be called and sustained to the Quorum of the Twelve Apostles, especially if this individual was nowhere near the area? To complicate the issue, the individual was to appear in Kirtland on an expected date to be ordained. Through the Church newspaper, of course. This is the position the Church and Orson Pratt found themselves in at the time of his call to the apostleship. The nomination was printed in the Church newspaper in Kirtland, *The Messenger and Advocate*. Elder Pratt at the time was serving a mission in central Ohio when, touched by the Spirit, he felt the need to speak to a man on the street. The man took Orson to his home, where *The Messenger and Advocate* happened to be lying there ready for him to read. When Orson read of his call, he immediately boarded a stage coach, traveled through the night, and arrived in Kirtland the next day at ten in the morning, April 26, 1835, on the requested appointed time and place.[8]

I've read numerous accounts of General Authorities and their calls. Not all knew prior to being sustained in conference of their appointment. At the April 1910 conference, Joseph Fielding Smith entered Temple Square on his way to the Tabernacle when a gatekeeper asked Brother Smith who the new apostle would be. Joseph Fielding responded that he could be sure that it wouldn't be him or the gatekeeper. It was interesting that as Joseph Fielding Smith was sitting in the Tabernacle, approximately thirty seconds prior to the naming of the new apostle, the Spirit confirmed to Brother Smith that it would be him. And it was.[9]

It was not uncommon for General Authorities to serve in more than one responsible position of leadership concurrently. For instance, Edward Hunter was called to serve as the presiding bishop in 1854 with Brigham Young and Heber C. Kimball as his counselors. In 1856, new counselors were selected for Bishop Hunter. Edward Hunter's first counselor was a man by the name of Leonard W. Hardy, who also happened to be bishop of the Salt Lake City Twelfth Ward, a position he would retain for the next twenty-one years.[10]

However, I think Marriner W. Merrill takes the cake. From 1899 to 1901 he was a member of the Council of the Twelve Apostles, the Logan Temple president, and stake president of the Cache Valley Stake.[11]

Today the Church employs a force of security people to protect our General Authorities. It hasn't always been this way. The following is from the diary of Joseph Fielding:

> At this time, strong attempts are making to take the Twelve. It seems as though earth and hell are made to see the work of the priesthood proceeding so rapidly. The United States Marshall has been here for some time searching and lying in wait for the Twelve and some others. He searched the [Nauvoo] temple through but in vain. The brethren have had to disguise themselves and conceal themselves to escape them. The charge is treason. You may see the Twelve, etc. wherever they go with six shooter pistols in their pockets, but thus far they have been preserved and are ministering in the [Nauvoo] temple and teaching the way of life and salvation.[12]

Regardless of the times, these men were ordained to their calls, chosen of the Lord. The fact that some may not have received the sustaining vote during conference in no way lessens their holy callings either as Apostles of the Lord Jesus Christ or other General Authorities. Again, the fact that one struggled with his language at the pulpit does not diminish the fact that he was called of God.

NOTES

1. josephsmithpapers.org
2. Paul Skousen, *The Skousen Book of Mormon World Records* (Springville, Utah: Cedar Fort, Inc., 2004), 220.

3. Lawrence R. Flake, *Prophets and Apostles of the Last Dispensation* (Provo, Utah: Religious Study Center, Brigham Young University, 2001), 178.
4. Richard S. Van Wagoner and Steven C. Walker, *A Book of Mormons* (Salt Lake City: Signature Books, 1982), 404, 412.
5. Andrew Jenson, *LDS Biographical Encyclopedia* (Salt Lake City: Publishers Press, 1901) 1:200.
6. Richard S. Van Wagoner and Steven C. Walker, *A Book of Mormons*, 164; See also Scott H. Partridge, ed., *The Thirteenth Apostle: The Diaries of Amasa M. Lyman*, 1832–1877 (Salt Lake City" Signature Books, 2016)
7. Richard S. Van Wagoner and Steven C. Walker, *A Book of Mormons*, 299.
8. Lawrence R. Flake, *Prophets and Apostles of the Last Dispensation*, 371–372.
9. Edited by Leonard J. Arrington, *The Presidents of the Church* (Salt Lake City, Utah: Deseret Book, 1986), 325.
10. Donald Q. Cannon and David J. Whittaker, *Supporting Saints: Life Stories of Nineteenth-Century Mormons* (Salt Lake City: Bookcraft Inc., 1985), 278).
11. Leon R. Hartshorn, *Exceptional Stories from the Lives of Early Apostles* (Provo, Utah: Spring Creek Book Company, 2004), 107.
12. Joseph Fielding, Diary (1843–1846), Church Archives in "They Might Have Known That He Was Not a Fallen Prophet"—The Nauvoo Journal of Joseph Fielding," transcribed and edited by Andrew F. Ehat, *BYU Studies* 19 (Winter 1979).

Groups

The following is from Mosiah Hancock in reference to a group he associated with in Nauvoo known as the Sons of Helaman. Mosiah was born in 1834 and would have been a pre-teen during the Nauvoo years of the Church. The Sons of Helaman, according to Mosiah, was a training for young boys to ready them for the Nauvoo Legion:

> We boys in Nauvoo formed a company called the "Sons of Helaman". Brother Baily from Massachusetts was our captain; and he was proud of us and we were proud of him. I was second Lieutenant, and

> we drilled quite a lot. Just before we left Nauvoo, I was in the Prophet's guard most of the time. I loved to march and parade and have the martial spirit; and was happy under military discipline. I would take my rifle with me even though not in company nor on parade with the Sons of Helaman. Often I was in the rank of the grown men, and no one ever said, "Your in the way". Why it was thus, I could never comprehend. I loved to see a martial feeling cultivated."[1]

The Nauvoo Legion continued through to Utah Territory. However, I fail to find information indicating that the Sons of Helaman also continued to the Salt Lake Valley. It appears that this was a Nauvoo group only. The fact that Mosiah refers to "Brother Baily" as his captain suggests to me that the formation of this group may have been at the instigation of Brother Baily. Nowhere do I find additional information from other sources referring to this group.

Again, the following quote is from Mosiah Hancock in reference to a Nauvoo based group that he associated with known as the Whistling and Whittling band. Mosiah does a great job explaining in his autobiography the group's purpose. This, too, was Nauvoo-based only. Nowhere do I read the services of the same group on the streets of Salt Lake City:

> I joined the whistling and whittling band. In those days there was, now and then, a fop or dude who would go to a man's shingle pile, and with his hat or cap cocked on one side, would sit and whittle and whistle. There was no law against that, but from what we could learn, some of them were interested in taking the life of the Prophet. We kept a good watch, and were directed to keep an eye on the "Black Ducks". We really tried to do our duty and we succeeded in bagging some game. I was about to give some instances, but forbear by saying, "In no case did I ever help to engage in whittling any one down to make them cross the great river unless they were known to be lurking around the Prophet's premises quite late, or to be seeking that which was none of their business. In extreme cases when we knew a man to be a snobber, and who still sought the life of the Prophet, we would use our rail. We generally had four boys to a rail—the rail would be flat on the bottom and was three cornered; on the top corner it was terribly sharp—fixed to suit the aggravating circumstances. Four boys generally knew how to manage the rail. We all had our knives and our timbers to whittle and make rails from, and we knew what tunes to whistle. I do not know if the boys from Nauvoo would

> like for me to betray those old-fashioned secrets; but that was the way we initiated those who seemed to wish with all their hearts to become thoroughly acquainted with the secrets of the Prophet.[2]

In the *Journal of Mormon History,* Jeffrey David Mahas shares his study, "I Intend to Get Up a Whistling School": "The Nauvoo Whistling and Whittling Movement, American Vigilante Tradition, and Mormon Theocratic Thought, indicates that even though there were younger participants, such as Mosiah Hancock shares above, for the most part, those belonging to the Whistling and Whittling gangs were in fact men."[3]

What appears on the more innocent side in Mosiah's description was in truth the activities of an organized vigilante group. Since the men belonging to this group were termed deacons, it may be assumed by some that these were kids. As you will soon read in the section on priesthood, men held the office of deacon during the Nauvoo years of the Church, up to and including in Utah Territory, when in 1877 the Aaronic Priesthood was then given to the younger boys. It was in April of 1845 when Brigham Young put a stop to the Whistling and Whittling movements activities in part due to the fears that the younger boys could be hurt, that "the inexperienced youths might target strangers who came to the city to conducting legitimate business," and also because of the damaging perception the older men in this group were giving to the non-members of the Church."[4]

• • •

The Prophet Joseph Smith organized a group known as the Council of Fifty. The name of the group is associated with the fact that fifty individuals claimed membership. At the time of the initial organization, there were twenty-two members of the group and others were added, including three non-members. The primary purpose was to search for a location for the Saints to flee to as they planned to leave the United States and prepare a government that could function until the Second Coming of Christ. In the short term they were also tasked with promoting Joseph Smith's presidential campaign for the 1844 presidential election.[5] They also discussed uniting the western tribes and petitioning Washington for authority to protect emigrants on the trail west. Anything the Council of Fifty did was for the benefit of the temporal lives of the Saints. Nowhere does it indicate that their purpose was spiritual; it was strictly secular.[6]

Brigham Young supplies us with additional information on the role of the Council of Fifty. It was Joseph Smith's vision to have this council seek redress for the wrongs committed to the Saints during the Missouri years of the Church. Ever since the expulsion from Jackson and surrounding counties, various efforts were launched for the reimbursements of lands, homes, animals and personal belongings lost. In this regard, memorials to Congress were prepared. The prophet was also interested in the council to seek a home for the Saints, a permanent dwelling where the members of the Lord's Church could reside in peace and "enjoy their religious rights."[7]

The following entry from William Huntington is in reference to a group known as the Living Constitution during the Nauvoo years. The Living Constitution was another name for the Council of Fifty:

> Monday, February 17, [1845], the Saints in Nauvoo were all called together. [The] weather [was] pleasant. The object of the meeting was made known by W.W. Phelps. It was to organize the temporal affairs of the Church. Twelve men were chosen [and] called the living constitution. These twelve chose three of the Twelve Apostles; John Taylor, George A. Smith and Amasa Lyman to preside over the temporal affairs of all the Church. Those men were appointed by the Church without a dissenting voice. Able addresses were delivered by the Twelve on the temporal affairs of the Church. [They] urged the necessity of becoming one in feeling and in action in temporal things as well as spiritual.[8]

The following is in reference to the time the Council of Fifty was fully complete on April 18, 1844: "At 9 met in Council. This day President Joseph [Smith] introduced J[oseph] W. Coolidge and D[avid] S. Hollister and added L[yman] Wight's name, and then declared the council full." This was also referred to as the "Kingdom of God."[9]

Other names for the Council of Fifty were the Special Council and the General Council. It was Joseph Smith who used these other titles.[10]

• • •

The Prophet Joseph Smith organized the Relief Society in Nauvoo, Illinois, on March 17, 1842 with Emma Smith as president.

Two years to the day, the last meeting of the Relief Society was held and then disbanded until Brigham Young called for the reorganization in 1867. What's intriguing is that attempts were made by various groups of women to reorganize. In 1854, the sisters formed what was sometimes referred to as Indian Relief Societies. These were formed in twenty-four Utah Territory wards. These relief societies were so called due to the mandate to serve the local native population. This was accomplished generally through the sewing of clothing for native women and children.[11]

• • •

During the Brigham Young years, it was common among the Saints to refer to non-members of the Church as Gentiles. The fact that the Saints applied this label to those not associating with the Church in no way constitutes an organized group. However, ironically, it was the population of those not belonging to The Church of Jesus Christ of Latter-day Saints in Utah Territory that preferred the use of this title to distinguish themselves as a group.[12]

I love to index genealogical records and discovered that on some Church and territorial census records, notations were made by the census takers referring to the inhabitants as "Gentile," "Apostate," or "Josephite [RLDS] Mormon." By the twentieth century, use of the titles dropped. The purpose of the Church separating itself from such contentious labels was to increase its public perception.[13]

NOTES

1. Autobiography of Mosiah Hancock, Typescript, BYU-S; boap.org/
2. Ibid.
3. Jeffrey David Mahas, "I Intend to Get Up a Whistling School": The Nauvoo Whistling and Whittling Movement, American Vigilante Tradition, and Mormon Theocratic Thought, *The Journal of Mormon History,* October 2017, 57.
4. Ibid., 62.
5. Coke Newell, *Latter Days* (St. Martin Press, New York City: 2000), 110–11.
6. Ronald K. Esplin, "Understanding the Council of Fifty and its Minutes," *BYU Studies*, Vol. 55, No. 3, 20–21.
7. Hyrum L. Andrus, "Joseph Smith and the West," *BYU Studies,* Issue 2, 1960, 137–38.

8. Autobiography of William Huntington, Typescript, Harold B. Lee Library, Brigham Young University.
9. Jedediah S. Rogers, ed., *The Council of Fifty* (Salt Lake City, Utah: Signature Books, 2014), 55, 57.
10. Hyrum L. Andrus, ibid.
11. Plewe, Brandon S., et. at., *Mapping Mormonism* (Provo, Utah: Brigham Young University Press, 2012) 102.
12. Ibid., 112, 124.
13. Ibid.

The book titled *The Council of Fifty* in the sources above is great resource to read the day by day minutes of their meetings.

Hospitals

When the Saints first arrived in the Salt Lake Valley, it was still part of Mexico. It was not until July 4, 1848, with the implementation of the Treaty of Guadalupe Hidalgo ending the war with Mexico that the valley became an unincorporated part of US territory. More than two years passed before Congress finally formally organized Utah Territory on September 9, 1850. During the years before there was a federal organization, Latter-day Saints had to organize themselves if they saw a need. For example, there was a high death rate in the Saints' settlements. Utah Territory had the highest death rate in 1849 than any other state in the Union, at one death per forty-eight people. This, in large part, was due to exposure to the elements by living in tents, wagons, and overcrowded structures.[1] Understanding this, a Council of Health was created. The *History Journal* on February 21, 1849 states, "Willard Richards had a medical conference in his wagon in the afternoon; similar meetings had been held during the past three or four weeks."[2]

Other leaders serving on this Council of Health were Heber C. Kimball and Albert Carrington.

The same could be said for the hospital situation in Utah. Before the Deseret Hospital became a reality on August 1, 1882, the Saints were required to use either St. Mark's Hospital, an Episcopalian facility, or the Catholic hospital, the Holy Cross. Brigham Young approached Eliza R. Snow with a proposal to head up a committee entitled the Deseret Hospital Association to study the feasibility to either purchase or construct a hospital.[3]

Today, members of the Church serve as politicians, businessmen, doctors, and lawyers who head up organizations, but not at the insistence of our Church leaders, rather, at the Church's encouragement. Today such committees are politically, municipally, or community driven.

NOTES

1. Lesson Committee, *Museum Memories-Daughters of Utah Pioneers* (Salt Lake City, Talon Printing, 2010), 2:82–83.
2. Ibid.
3. Ibid., 2:86.

Institute of Religion

I like the institute of religion. I mean, I really like it. Let me explain. Shortly after my mission I enrolled in an institute class. Class had just ended. I was putting all my notes together and getting ready for the walk home, when I noticed a pretty young lady standing beside my desk decked out in a ski outfit. I recognized her as a young lady in our ward. In fact, I had talked to her for a moment at a young adult activity a week or two previous. It was winter time, hence the young lady wearing a snow suit. As I was bundling up for the jaunt up the street to home, she asked me if I wanted a ride. I told her I'd be fine. She reminded me it was cold outside and starting to snow. I'm not the brightest crayon in the box, but I caught the hint. "Sure, why not?" And I'm glad I did because forty years later, even though I do most of the driving, she will still occasionally drive on a cold day.

Anyway, I'm off course. Here's a question. Has the institute of religion that you would find on college and university campuses today always been known as the institute of religion? I would have said yes, but have since discovered that the institute of religion actually began in 1970. What was the predecessor to it then? It was known as the Deseret Clubs, which operated until 1970, at which time they were dissolved.[1]

NOTE

1. Berrett, William Edwin, *The Restored Church* (Salt Lake City: Deseret Book Company, 1973), 307.

Marriages During the Utah War Crisis

When news of the federal army approaching Utah Territory initially reached the ears of Brigham Young as the Saints were celebrating the tenth anniversary of their entrance into these valleys, the wheels started spinning in his mind. Measures were taken to protect the Saints. To be successful, President Young knew it was essential for able-bodied young men to be called to hinder the entrance of Johnston's army into Salt Lake City. Prior to the deployment of these young men, Brigham Young counseled those that were not married to take wives. One such young man was John Moyes, who married seventeen-year-old Elizabeth (last name not given).[1]

Brigham Young's counsel didn't apply to the young people only, but also extended to the widows. With the approach of Johnston's army, widow Abigail Cadwallader Brown, obedient to the prophet's counsel, married Ben Brown, although she never lived with him. With time the marriage was annulled and Abigail was later sealed to Abia William Brown.[2]

NOTES

1. Lesson Committee, *Museum Memories-Daughters of Utah Pioneers* (Salt Lake City, Talon Printing, 2010), 2:9.
2. Ibid., 1:376.

Meetinghouses

As long as I can remember, the Barkers have been creatures of habit. My parents always, and I mean always, arrived approximately ten minutes prior to the opening of sacrament meeting and nestled in the east end of the last middle pew. We arrived early enough that it was a non-issue staking ownership of the same pew each Sunday. Judging by those who occupied other pews, we weren't far different from a number of other families in the ward. It became obvious to me during my young life that early arrivals had a tendency of claiming the same favored pew.

In most cases, during the early Utah Territory years, families didn't have a choice of where they sat. No, it wasn't assigned seating, or a case of latecomers sitting on the front pew, but rather each family was required to construct and provide their own bench.

In Tooele "the first public house was built in 1854." John Alexander Bevan recalled the following:

> The head of each family made a bench for his family to sit on. These benches were usually made of slabs, with four legs put in on the round side of the slab. . . . Besides the fire for light, they had tallow candles, home-made, and each family was supposed to furnish a candle. The house was used for all purposes, both religious and otherwise. It was the schoolhouse, the meeting house, and the amusement hall. It had a pulpit on the west side near the center. This pulpit, or stand, was about large enough to hold three men.[1]

In some towns during the 1800s in Utah, segregating female from males was common in meetinghouses. This practice continued for a time, at least until 1867. This may have been more of a ward by ward or stake by stake practice.[2]

NOTES

1. Ronald W. Walker and Doris R. Dant ed., *Nearly Everything Imaginable* (Provo, Utah: BYU Press, 1999), 254.
2. Davis Bitton, "Early Mormon Lifestyles; on the Saints as Human

Beings," in *The Restoration Movement: Essays in Mormon History,* ed. F. Mark McKiernan, Alma R. Blair, and Paul M. Edwards (Lawrence, Kans.: Coronado Press, 1973), 298–302. In Ronald W. Walker and Doris R. Dant ed., *Nearly Everything Imaginable*, 256–57.

Meetings

Currently, at the close of our sacrament meetings, after the last talk is given or testimony borne, a hymn is sung and then an assigned individual closes the meeting with prayer. This wasn't always the format in the Church. Prior to and during the Kirtland years, when the Saints met in the temple, and if Joseph Smith Sr. was conducting the meeting, it was not unusual for all to be on their knees at the conclusion of the meeting, whispering quietly personal, vocal prayers.[1]

It was also during the later Kirtland years that fast and testimony meetings were held on the first Thursday of each week. The Saints were given a choice of which fast and testimony meeting they desired to attend. Choices of 10 a.m. and 4 p.m. were provided and again, conducted by Patriarch Joseph Smith Sr. Other meetings in the temple were the regular Sunday meetings, priesthood meetings during the week, and school classes also during the week.[2]

Brigham Young shares the history of the fast day:

> You know that the first Thursday in each month we hold as a fast day. How many here know the origin of this day? Before tithing was paid, the poor were supported by donations. They came to Joseph and wanted help, in Kirtland, and he said there should be a fast day, which was decided upon. It was to be held once a month, as it is now, and all that would have been eaten that day, of flour, or meat, or fruit, or anything else, was to be carried to the fast meeting and put into the hands of a person selected for the purpose of taking care of it and distributing it among the poor.[3]

The Thursday fast meetings continued for a number of years when the Saints first entered the Salt Lake Valley. If fast day was held on Thursdays back then, why don't we continue this practice today? It wasn't until December 6, 1896, when the First Presidency put an end to this practice. The reason the practice ended I'm sure is obvious. It became too hard for employers to let their employees leave early.[4] Also, with time, the population of those that considered themselves members of The Church of Jesus Christ of Latter-day Saints in Utah watered down over the years. More and more outsiders moved in, and more and more businesses were operated and owned by those that were not of our faith and did not have the same understanding of our religious beliefs, rituals, and culture. A letter from missionary Hyrum Mack Smith to his apostle father, Joseph F. Smith, while he served a mission in England, ultimately led to the change of Fast meeting from Thursdays to Sundays. Hyrum argued that the English Saints had to ask for the time off work. This time off came at a loss of compensation. He said, depending on vocation, it was necessary for men to wash and change, which led to additional loss of time. Let's face it, not all Saints could afford to miss even part of a day of work.[5]

Presiding Bishop Edward Hunter lamented the fact that the first Thursday of the month fast meeting was poorly attended. Another bishop stated that the Saints should be allowed to leave their places of work to attend. Bishop Leonard W. Hardy, counselor to Bishop Edward Hunter, believed that those who did not attend their fast meeting should have to pay double fast offering.[6]

• • •

In 1891, Nickel Sunday was instituted. One Sunday a year, Sunday School students, teachers, and officers would bring a nickel as a contribution to the Sunday School budget. Nickel Sunday was replaced with Dime Sunday and then Budget Fund Sunday.[7]

• • •

Humor over the pulpit during meetings conducted in The Church of Jesus Christ of Latter-day Saints is not unusual, whether in our own ward meetings or during general conference. The same was true during the early Church. Many are familiar with the tales (real or not) associated with J. Golden Kimball. Even earlier than this was the unexpected antics of George A. Smith. On one occasion, while speaking in a very hot tabernacle, Elder Smith removed his wig to wipe the sweat off his face to the delight of those Saints in attendance. I don't know if this is the type of humor you would expect today. Nonetheless, humor over the pulpit has always been appreciated by the Saints of all ages.[8]

• • •

During the pioneer Church, quality of meetings was a problem. One issue dealt with the few speakers called on since women generally didn't speak in meetings and attendance was usually sub-par. This situation led to too much repetition and boring meetings. Provo Saint Sidney Alexander Pace shares the following: "We were in the habit of going into meeting on Sunday and if the speaker was not lively enough, fifteen or twenty of us young boys would get up and walk out of meeting and go down by Bishop Loveless's home. . . . They used to have large straw stacks and here we went to have our fun."[9]

Understanding the issue, Angus M. Cannon's directive from the General Authorities was to implement the home missionary program in 1877, a program which no longer exists in the Church. The idea of the home missionaries, in a sense, were similar to the stake high counselors visiting and speaking in the wards today. Much emphasis was placed on the person's ability to speak, and all ward missionaries were instructed to give interesting talks.[10]

• • •

A practice performed inside the temples today, the prayer circle, was a practice performed at the ward level during Utah Territory period to the early 1900s. Not just any member could attend the prayer circle. In fact, membership was exclusive in many instances. At first, those invited met two Sundays of each month in a room at the meetinghouse. With time this practice was reduced to fast meetings. Regarding attendance, John W. Welch stated: "There were too many vacant chairs in our prayer circled room and [we] felt that some of our brethren remained away without any excuse. We meet here for our own good and also for what good we can do to others" (Sunday, November 1, 1908).[11]

To belong, a Saint invited to the group was expected to be a full tithe payer and obey the Word of Wisdom. Most were able to account for their tithing. However, not everyone was as strict in obeying the Lord's law of heath. Nonetheless, this was typical of those times as you will soon discover in the section on the Word of Wisdom.[12]

• • •

Brigham Young, like Joseph Smith, believed that any minister wanting to preach to the Saints be afforded this luxury. Brigham Young once said the following to the Saints in Ogden in 1871: "Accord to every reputable person who may visit you, and who may wish to occupy the stands of your meeting houses to preach to you the privilege of doing so, no matter whether he be a Catholic, Presbyterian, Congregationalist, Baptist."[13]

As part of this claim of religious toleration, Father Scanlan, of the Roman Catholic faith, was provided the St. George tabernacle, during which "Peter's Mass" was sung by members of The Church of Jesus Christ of Latter-day Saints in Latin.[14]

Doctrine and Covenants 46: 2–6 reads:

> But notwithstanding those things which are written, it always had been given to the elders of my church from the beginning, and ever shall be, to conduct all meetings as they are directed and guided by the Holy Spirit.
>
> Nevertheless ye are commanded never to cast any one out from your public meetings, which are held before the world.
>
> Ye are also commanded not to cast any one who belongeth to the church out of your sacrament meetings; nevertheless, if any have trespassed, let him not partake until he makes reconciliation.
>
> And again I say unto you, ye shall not cast any out of your sacrament meetings who are earnestly seeking the kingdom—I speak this concerning those who are not of the church.
>
> And again I say unto you, concerning your confirmation meetings, that if there be any that are not of the church, that are earnestly seeking after the kingdom, ye shall not cast them out.

• • •

Those baptized into the Church are on some occasions given the gift of the Holy Ghost during the same meeting shortly after they are baptized. However, some received the gift of the Holy Ghost during sacrament meeting. Today, we don't refer to this as a confirmation meeting the way the Doctrine and Covenants speaks of it and the way Fanny Stenhouse mentions the confirmation meeting during her time.

During a confirmation meeting, the bestowal of the gift of the Holy Ghost was different from our current practice. Fanny writes that those who were baptized during the week and wished confirmation were asked to come to the front, after which three elders placed their hands on the head of the individual and pronounced the following blessing:

> Martha; by virtue of the authority vested in us, we confirm you a member of the Church of Jesus Charis of Latter-day Saints; and as you have been obedient to the teachings of the Elders, and have gone down into the waters of baptism for the remission of your sins, we confer upon you the Gift of the Holy Ghost, that it may abide with you forever, and be a lamp unto your feet, and a light upon your pathway, leading an guiding you into all truth. This blessing we confirm upon your head, in the name of the Father, and of the Son, and of the Holy Ghost. Amen.

After the first elder concluded with the confirmation, the next elder then provided a second blessing:

> He spoke for some time with extreme earnestness, when suddenly he was seized with a nervous trembling which was quite perceptible, and which evidently betokened intense mental or physical excitement. He began to prophecy great things for this sister in the future, and in solemn and mysterious language proclaimed the wonders which God would perform for her sake.[15]

• • •

John Corrill, during his investigation of the gospel, was certain to "detect their hypocrisy" during the Church's meetings. It may seem odd to us today, but it was not unusual during the early years of the Church to have meetings last throughout the night. John was in attendance at one such meeting. His purpose was to detect hypocrisy, but discovered something unexpected when he stated, "The meeting lasted all night, and such a meeting I never attended before." Corrill further states, "I watched closely and examined carefully, every movement of the meeting, and after exhausting all my powers to find the deception, I was obliged to acknowledge, in my own mind that the meeting had been inspired by some supernatural agency."[16]

In 1907, while being raised in the Cardston, Alberta area, Hugh B. Brown, provides us with a glimpse of his meeting schedule during the week, which most likely was typical for most members at the time: "Monday, priesthood meeting, Tuesday, M.I.A. preparation class, Wednesday choir practice."[17]

NOTES

1. Starting in 1877 and continuing through to 1979, quarterly stake conferences were the norm.
2. Edward W. Tullidge, *The Women of Mormondom* (New York, 1877), 207–10, 213.
3. James B. Allen and Glen M. Leonard, *The Story of the Latter-day Saints* (Salt Lake City: Deseret Book, 1992), 111.
4. Brigham Young, December 8, 1867, in *Journal of Discourses*, Vol. 12, 116.
5. Dean A. Wengreen, "The Origin and History of the Fast Day in The Church of Jesus Christ of Latter-day Saints, 1830–1896." Master's thesis, Brigham Young University, 1955.
6. Jerry H. Houck, *Witnesses of Christ: Prophets and Apostles of our Dispensation* (Cedar Fort: Springville, Utah, 2015), 165–166.
7. Ronald W. Walker and Doris R. Dant ed., *Nearly Everything Imaginable (*Provo, Utah: BYU Press, 1999), 257–58.
8. history.churchofjesuschrist.org/article/things-you-didnt-know-about-sunday-school?lang=eng
9. Arnold K. Garr et al., *Encyclopedia of Latter-day Saint History* (Salt Lake City: Deseret Book, 2000), 1114.
10. Ronald W. Walker and Doris R. Dant ed., *Nearly Everything Imaginable,* 255.
11. Donald Q. Cannon and David J. Whittaker, *Supporting Saints: Life Stories of Nineteenth-Century Mormons* (Salt Lake City: Bookcraft Inc., 1985), 381–82.
12. Ronald W. Walker and Doris R. Dant ed., *Nearly Everything Imaginable,* 465.
13. Ibid., 465.

14. J. Keith Melville, "Theory and Practice of Church and State During the Brigham Young Era," *BYU Studies,* Issue 1, 1961, 54.
15. Rebecca Bartholomew, *Audacious Women—Early British Mormon Immigrants* (Signature Books: Salt Lake City, 1995), 71–72.
16. John Corrill, *A Brief History of the Church of Christ of Latter Day Saints (Commonly Called Mormons, Including an Account of their Doctrine and Discipline, with the Reasons of the Author for Leaving the Church)* (St. Louis, n.p., 1839).
17. Martha Sonntag Bradley and Mary Brown Firmage Woodward, *4 Zinas* (Signature Books: Salt Lake City, 2000), 392.

Military

Today's Church would be hard-pressed to provide a legitimate reason for an organized militia similar to the Nauvoo Legion. We live in a different day and age, and are no longer physically persecuted on a wide scale the way the Church experienced shortly after its organization and through much of the 1800s. I seriously doubt federal troops will be dispatched to the global center of the Church in Salt Lake City. It just isn't going to happen. Nevertheless, there was a time and place when a militia was required. Saints in the Church are more than aware of the Nauvoo Legion, which served in both Illinois and Utah. However, what might not be understood is that boys as young as thirteen to men as old as seventy-five belonged to this military body.[1]

NOTE

1. Richard E. Bennett, Susan Easton Black, Donald Q. Cannon, *The Nauvoo Legion in Illinois: A History of the Mormon Militia, 1841–1846* (Norman, Oklahoma: The Arthur H. Clark Company, 2010), 385.

Ministering (Home/Visiting Teaching)

The phrases "home teaching" and "visiting teaching" are a thing of the past. Today, due to the instructions from a prophet of God, we now minister. It's interesting that other denominations are familiar with the term "ministering." In fact, we utilized the term before we adopted the phrase. But then, it hadn't always been home teaching either, which didn't become the phrase of use until sometime in the 1960s. Starting in 1908, the typical nomenclature applied to such activity was the ward teachers and anything prior to this was referred to as teachers, acting teachers, or block teachers. The term "block teacher" originated from the Utah Territory years when a companionship was assigned to families residing in one square block. It wasn't just the terminology that was overhauled through the decades, but also the method.[1]

Today we're accustomed to a Melchizedek Priesthood brother minister to families along with a teacher or priest in the Aaronic Priesthood, or another member of the higher priesthood. This wasn't always the case. There were times in the early Utah Church when teachers, priests, or members of the Melchizedek Priesthood were assisted by a deacon. In fact, this responsibility was laid on the shoulders of the teachers quorum during the Missouri years, but shifted to the priests once the Saints settled in Nauvoo. This may seem like a huge burden to place on the shoulders of a young man. However, as you are about to discover in the section on the priesthood, the age of the individuals that we refer to as a deacon, teacher, or priest today wasn't the same during the Palmyra to the mid-Utah Territory (1877) years in the Church.

Today, we're comfortable visiting about four families. During the Missouri, Nauvoo, and Utah Territory years of the Church, a companionship could be expected to visit eight to twenty families.[2]

Similarly, like today, in many wards, the companionships during the pioneer Church were expected to visit their families once a month. However, in other areas of Utah Territory the stipulation was quarterly or "randomly." Also like today, too many ministers put this responsibility off until the last day of the month. In 1864, Bishop Hardy, a counselor in the presiding bishopric, complained about men who "put off their visits through the wards to the very last evening before they have to give in their report, this hurrying way of visiting, failed to accomplish the design of a teachers duty."[3]

The following is William Cahoon's reminiscence of his first visit as a home teacher to the Prophet Joseph Smith and his family:

> Before I close my testimony concerning this good man (Joseph Smith), I wish to mention one circumstance which I shall never forget. I was called and ordained to act as a ward teacher to visit the families of the Saints. I got along very well until I was obliged to pay a visit to the Prophet. Being young, only 17 years of age, I felt my weakness in the capacity of a teacher. I almost felt like shrinking from my duty.
>
> Finally, I went to the door and knocked and in a minute the Prophet came to the door. I stood there trembling and said to him; 'Brother Joseph, I have come to visit you in the capacity of a ward teacher, if it is convenient for you.' He said, 'Brother William, come right in. I am glad to see you. Sit down in the chair there and I will go and call my family in.' They soon came in and took seats. The Prophet said, "Brother William, I submit myself and family into your hands," and took his seat. "Now, Brother William," said he, "Ask all the questions you feel like."
>
> By this time my fears and trembling had ceased and I said, "Brother Joseph, are you trying to live your religion?" He answered, "Yes." I then said, "Do you pray in your family?" He answered "Yes." "Do you teach your family the principles of the gospel?" He replied, "Yes, I am trying to do it." "Do you ask a blessing on your food?" He said he did. "Are you trying to live in peace and harmony with all your family?" He said he was.
>
> I turned to Sister Emma, his wife, and said, "Sister Emma, are you trying to live your religion? Do you teach your children to obey their parents? Do you try to teach them to pray?" To all these questions she answered, "Yes, I am trying to do so." I then turned to Joseph and said, "I am now through with my questions as a teacher and now if you have any instructions to give, I shall be happy to receive them." He said, "God bless you Brother William, and if you are humble and faithful you shall have power to settle all difficulties that may come before you in the capacity of a teacher." I then left my parting blessing upon him and his family, as a teacher, and departed.[4]

From the journal of Emmeline B. Wells, on Thursday August 27, 1874, we discover the name of the fore runner to visiting teaching: "Little Lou's twelfth birthday. I was taken very sick in the morning continued very bad all day long. I suffered the most agonizing pain got a little easier towards evening. The Lady teachers called."[5]

With the Relief Society disbanded in Nauvoo prior to the Saints being pushed out, this in no way hindered the sisters from organizing "visiting rounds" during their stay in Winter Quarters. The sisters not only visited, but took an active part in the healing of other sick women and children assisted those close to giving childbirth, and held prayer circles.[6]

NOTES

1. Rex A. Anderson, "A Documentary History of the Lord's Way of Watching over the Church by the Priesthood through the Ages." Master's thesis, Brigham Young University, 1974; Gary L. Phelps, "Home Teaching—Attempts by the Latter-day Saints to Establish an Effective Program during the Nineteenth Century." Master's thesis, Brigham Young University, 1975.
2. Rex A. Anderson, "A Documentary History of the Lord's Way of Watching over the Church by the Priesthood through the Ages."; Gary L. Phelps, "Home Teaching—Attempts by the Latter-day Saints to Establish an Effective Program during the Nineteenth Century."
3. Ronald W. Walker and Doris R. Dant ed., *Nearly Everything Imaginable (*Provo, Utah: BYU Press, 1999), 261–62.
4. "Autobiography (1813–1878)" in Stella Shurtleff and Brent Farrington Cahoon eds., *Reynolds Cahoon and His Stalwart Sons* (Salt Lake City: Paragon Press, 1960)
5. Kenneth W. Godfrey, Audrey M. Godfrey, and Jill Mulvay Derr, *Women's Voices: An Untold History of The Latter-day Saints 1830–1900* (Salt Lake City: Deseret Book Company, 1982), 295.
6. *History of the Saints,* Harley, William G., ed. (American Fork, Utah: Covenant Communications, 2012), 63.

Mission Calls

If given the choice today, it would be interesting to see where missionaries would serve. I'm not exactly sure why, but for whatever reason I wanted to serve in Australia. However, when I opened my call and read that the

Lord thought I should serve in the Massachusetts Boston Mission, it just felt right, and at that point on, no other mission mattered. Two short years later, as I boarded the plane for home, I understood better than ever why the Lord sent me to the best place He could have sent me.

Section 80 of the Doctrine and Covenants is a revelation directed to Stephen Burnett and his companion, Eden Smith. Verse 3 reads as follows: "Wherefore, go ye and preach my gospel, whether to the north or to the south, to the east or to the west, it mattereth not, for ye cannot go amiss."

This may seem like a special case, that the Lord had a special mission just for these two elders. However, such was not the case. In *History of the Church* I came across this:

> It may seem odd that the Lord left it up to the two missionaries where they desired to serve. But not really, as the fact below will attest.
>
> At a special conference of the Church on April 10, 1843, many elders received their mission calls. There were a few noteworthy calls:
>
> William B. Brink—the interior of Pennsylvania, where the elders have not been.
>
> Eleazar Willis—wherever he chose.
>
> Moses Wade—a county in New York where there had not been any preaching by the Saints.[1]

Again, from the *History of the Church*:

> At a conference of the Church, September 17, 1837, in Kirtland, Ohio another unique situation plays out where 109 elders number themselves and then split into eight groups of 13 missionaries each. Each group is designated a destination based on a point of the compass. Elders 105–109 are assigned a group and then all present are instructed if their call does not suit them, then they can trade with another elder from another group that will be more agreeable to their liking.[2]

Henry Bigler, of Mormon Battalion and the California gold rush fame (he was the first to record in his journal the first gold discovered in California, kicking off the gold rush), while traveling to Salt Lake City from Farmington on February 28, 1857, happened to meet Brigham Young on the road when President Young pulled his wagon alongside Brother Bigler and dropped a bombshell. He told Henry to prepare for a mission to the Sandwich Islands. Definitely more casual than formal, but the end result was the same.[3]

A number of years ago neighbors moved in across the street. Through visits, my wife and I became fast friends with them. It was interesting when the man told me about the mission he served during the 1960s. He said he wasn't called on a regular proselyting mission like most young men called during this time, but rather he was called as a Church building missionary. His call was to build church buildings, and so this is what he did for two years. Yes, such a mission did exist. It was in 1953 that the Church organized the Building Missionary Program. By the completion of this project in 1969, over 2,000 chapels were built around the world in such areas as Canada, the United States, Asia, and Latin America. Yes, these Church Building Missionaries constructed chapels. However, the New Zealand Temple was also constructed using the labors of these missionaries. As a point of interest, the Church resurrected the mission again in 2012, experimenting with the building of chapels in Africa.[4]

Church building missionaries may not seem so unusual. In fact, far from it. Most likely the strangest mission calls were those few missionaries called on gold mining missions by Brigham Young. In late 1849 approximately twenty such missionaries left Utah for the gold fields of California. Due to the lack of success, Elder Charles C. Rich then reassigned these same men to finish out their missions in the Sandwich Islands as proselyting missionaries.[5] George Q. Cannon was one of the young men called to serve on the gold mining mission. The following are his thoughts at the time of his call: "There was no place I would not rather have gone too at that time than California. I heartily despised the work of digging gold."[6]

Missionary Henry Bigler shares additional information on the call to leave this mission for the Sandwich Islands:

> Sunday, October 6th. Last Thursday morning we commenced taking out the gold after laboring so long in building and repairing our dam so often, and today we divided the pile, there being twelve shares, $200.00 apiece.
>
> Sunday, October 13th. Washing gold all week and today divided 444 dollars each.
>
> Tuesday, 15th the gold has failed, o what a pity.
>
> Wednesday, 16 divided 92 dollars apiece. We shall make preparations to leave for the Sandwich Islands forthwith.

The decision to go to the Sandwich Islands came as the result of an event that took place at "Slap Jack Bar," which more than justified the entire venture, as far as the Church was concerned. Bigler's record of this event reads as follows:

> This morning the brethren was called together at our tent by Bro. Rich, he stated that he wanted some of us to go on a mission to the Sandwich Islands to preach the gospel, that his opinion was that it would cost no more to spend the winter there than it would here, that we could make nothing in the wintertime in consequence of so much water in the streams, and another thing provisions would be much higher in the mines and it would cost us more money to stay here and make nothing than if we went to the islands and preach, in his opinion it would be the best thing we could do and the best council he could give . . . then he called upon ten of us 1 of which was to go to Oragon [Oregon] with Boyd Steward, and the remaining 9 was set apart as follow, Thomas Whittle, Thomas Morras, John Dixon, myself, Geo. Cannon, Wm. Farrer, John Berry if he wished, James Keeler , James Hawkins. He then laid his hands on us and set us apart for the mission and blessed us in the name of the Lord, and told us to act as the spirit dictated when we got there.[7]

A year prior to this event, Bigler recorded in his journal on October 16, 1849, at the time of his call to dig for gold in California: "Last night I dreamed I was not going for goal [gold] but was going to the islands to preach the gospel."[8] Later, Henry records, "Today Bro. Pratt asked me if I would go to the islands should Bros. Rich and Amasa Lyman call me to go. I told him that I should if that was their council."[9]

What was the dollar amount of gold discovered during the gold mining missions of 1848–51? Seventy-one thousand dollars were found to help boost Utah's economy.[10]

Yes, being called to labor as a gold mining missionary would seem completely unusual. However, another mission call in Utah Territory ranked up there with those sent to gather gold. When the Church first entered the valley, there was a shortage of many everyday items that the Saints were accustomed to purchasing while residing in the confines of the United States. As strange as it may seem, paper was high on this list of scarce commodities. Yes, paper was difficult to come by in Utah Territory, at least enough paper to fulfill the supply demands of the *Deseret News*. Members in the early Salt Lake Valley were out-of-the-box thinkers and consistently determined substitute materials for what was normally used. For instance, if there was a lack of sheep and wool to manufacture clothing, no problem, at least no problem to the Sisters in the Church. Buffalo fur caught on shrubs served as an adequate replacement, or if this wasn't enough, they shaved the family dog.[11] If thread was scarce, again, not a big deal. It's amazing how well horse tail or mane hair worked.[12]

With time those expected to produce a newspaper found an alternative—rags. In stating this, realize that the use of rags as a substitute for paper was not unique to the Church. This practice was in existence decades prior to the organization of the Church.[13] Yes, rags! They would print the paper on rags if paper was scarce. The *Deseret News* advertised on its pages, "RAGS! RAGS!! RAGS!!! Save your rags, everybody in Deseret save your rags; old wagon covers, tents, quilts, shirts, etc., etc., are wanted for paper."[14] I guess the ads failed to generate the required quota of rags to sustain the newspaper because Brigham Young called George Goddard on a rag mission. For over three years, Elder Goddard combed Utah into Idaho collecting rags. His activities were not confined to begging for rags from door to door, but also preaching rag sermons on Sundays from the pulpit. As it was, George Goddard's first rag speech was in the Tabernacle with follow up speeches from Brigham Young and Heber C. Kimball.[15]

• • •

George A. Smith was called to serve a mission at the age of twenty-one. Really nothing too odd about this at the time or currently. I'm sure this Church has seen plenty of young men called older than the standard age. But define standard age. Today we say eighteen to nineteen. However, in Brigham Young's day, there was no such thing as standard age. If you were in your mid-teens or older, you were fair game at general conference to have your name called over the pulpit. What might have been different is the length of George Albert Smith's mission. He was called for two-and-a-half months to travel through Utah and reactivate less active youth.[16]

George Albert Smith was not the only missionary called to a specific group. On December 22, 1875, Joseph Edward Taylor was called by Brigham Young to serve a mission in the states of Nebraska, Iowa, and Illinois to search out the "Josephites," those who had seceded from the Church at the death of the Prophet Joseph Smith and belonged to the Reorganized Church of Jesus Christ of Latter-day Saints (today known as the Community of Christ) and followers of Joseph Smith III. With the help of his two companions, Claudius V. Spencer and Isaac Bullock, the three missionaries were successful in inviting and baptizing thirty-six individuals into the Church.[17]

• • •

Charles Kingston is another such elder who received a special mission call at the hands of Lorenzo Snow when called to follow the line of the Union Pacific Railroad and make connections with the scattered Saints along the rail line. I imagine, because many of these people were separated from the main body of Saints in Utah, there was a high average of inactivity.[18]

Another interesting call is that of Thomas Fielding Burton and his companion, Louis D. King. They were called from their residence in Salt Lake City in 1901 to serve a Mutual Improvement mission to labor in the Alberta Stake. While in Canada, they worked with Elder John W. Taylor.[19]

• • •

In 1869, William Bell was called to serve a mission to teach woodworking in Heber City and establish a furniture shop.[20]

Other strange stuff that has happened concerning mission calls came from the life of Charles Arthur Welsch. Called to serve in the Southern States in 1883, he most likely was a little shocked when he was transferred in what may have been the Church's longest transfer. At the end of the transfer, he found himself in Great Britain.[21]

Then there was the call of Charles A. Callis to serve a two-year mission to the Southern States in 1906. After his return home, he was immediately called to serve as mission president of the Southern States Mission from 1908 to 1933. When finally released, he was then called into the Quorum of the Twelve.[22]

• • •

Many men were called to serve multiple missions, usually within months of each other. This was not uncommon. For instance, Matthias Foss Cowley was called as a nineteen-year-old to serve a two-year mission to the Southern States. At the completion of his mission he returned home only to be called to the same mission by President Wilford Woodruff five months later.[23]

Also common in the early Church was the speed at which men responded to the call. One of my missionary companions shared with me the time he was given to prepare prior to reporting to the mission home. He stated that his mouth dropped as he read his call, not so much from where he would serve, but rather the expected time to report to the mission home in Salt Lake City (That's right, not all Elders have reported to the MTC in Provo, Utah). He was given two weeks' noticed. But to be honest, to many of the early missionaries in Kirtland, Nauvoo, and Utah Territory, two weeks seemed like a lifetime. The example of Leman Copley serves well to prove this point. Leman, who originally belonged to the Shaker faith, visited Joseph Smith on May 7, 1831. It was during this visit when Joseph Smith received section 49 in our current Doctrine and Covenants. It was also at this time when Joseph called Leman Copley, along with Sidney Rigdon and Parley P. Pratt, on a mission to North Union, Ohio, thirty-five miles away from Kirtland. Later that evening, the threesome arrived among the Shakers in North Union and their ministry began.[24]

• • •

Amasa Lyman, in the early 1840s, moved his family to Nauvoo, occupying part of a house belonging to Brother Osmyn M. Duel, and worked with Brother Theodore Turley in his shop repairing guns. Thus engaged for a short time, when Brother Charles Shumway, from northern Illinois, called on Brother Joseph for elders to go home with him to preach in that country. The Prophet sent him to Elder Lyman, with directions that he should go. The steamer on which they were to go was insight when Brother Lyman received word of his mission. Amasa went home, one mile distant, took leave of his family, and was at the landing as the boat rounded to depart. He preached in the region of Galena, and in Wisconsin, until

October, when he returned to Nauvoo, when he arrived on the last day of the conference. During the conference he was appointed a mission to the city of New York.[25]

• • •

Throughout Church history there has been an overabundance of various missions that an elder could be called to. The same applied for entire families living in the Salt Lake area. Families were called to various missions throughout Utah Territory, California, Mexico, Arizona, and Nevada much the same way the elders were called. There wasn't a family that entered the Tabernacle for general conference without the thought tucked away in the back of their mind that they just might be called to serve. Hundreds of calls were extended over the pulpit to both elders and families. To some it was a non-issue. Picking up and leaving, if it was the prophet's will, was never a question. On the other hand, there were some who refused to leave the comforts of Salt Lake City to serve in some outlying area on the fringes of civilization. Some such missions that families were called to, believe it or not, were a wine mission. Others included a lead mission, wool mission, the muddy mission, the silk mission, the cotton mission, the sugar mission, the flax mission, and the iron mission.[26]

There is an innumerable supply of stories of those who opened their mouths and then let the Lord work the miracle. I imagine anyone who has served a mission can attest to this. Samuel Smith, the first missionary of the Church, comes to mind. He opened his mouth, but yet felt very much a failure. I'm sure he's chuckling now, simply because I'm certain the Book of Mormon he left with a Methodist minister, John P. Greene, that was eventually passed on to Brigham Young, who eventually shared it with Heber C. Kimball is now responsible for tens of thousands of baptisms, possibly even in the hundreds of thousands.

One of my favorite stories of opening one's mouth and preaching the gospel is the story of Eli H. Pierce. Today when we watch general conference we fully expect temples to be announced and are filled with anticipation when the prophet takes the podium. Back in the mid- to late-1880s, men entered the Tabernacle during conference time, not with the thought of what temples would be built, but rather whose names were going to be called over the pulpit to serve missions. Eli H. Pierce was one of the names announced on October 5, 1875, except that Eli was not in the congregation. Eli would be the first to admit the reason he wasn't at conference was that he had no desire to be there. He was less active, and that's the way he preferred it. He was a railroad man who bought cigars like they were going out of style (although the Word of Wisdom at this time was not a matter of temple worthiness, and it was not uncommon for many Saints to indulge in substances that we now considered in violation of this commandment) and had never read more than a few pages of scripture in his lifetime. One of his fellow work associates heard the call and immediately telegraphed Eli the message. When the telegraph arrived, Eli was smoking a pipe and reading a novel. He states that after reading the call, he threw the novel in the waste basket (and has never picked up one since), got rid of the pipe, was re-baptized, ordained a Seventy, and in one month from the time of the call was serving his mission in the state of New York. Brother Pierce said, "Remarkable as it may seem . . . a thought of disregarding the call, or of refusing to comply with the requirement, never once entered my mind." In fact, Eli would go on and serve three more missions. Here's a rundown of the numbers he accumulated, only because he knew if he opened his mouth the Lord would bless him: baptisms, 108; ordinations, 11; children blessed, 37; branches organized, 5; branches reorganized, 1; marriages, 1; meetings held, 249; miles traveled, 9,870; total cost, $1,320.[27]

At the time of my call to serve in New England, I noticed that my mission president was fairly new in the field. I realized I would serve my entire two years under one mission president. However, this wasn't the case. I discovered fast that when the Church needed an individual in another calling, the fact that he was a mission president wasn't going to stop those plans. When I had five months remaining in the field, we said our farewells to each other. The same was true for some of the early missionaries. George Henry Crosby was called to serve in the Southern States Mission in 1867, but after serving for a brief stint in the field was called home to Utah to serve in the bishopric, a calling he held for thirty-two years.[28]

There were others called to serve missions . . . as a bishop. The following is from the life of Franklin Wheeler Young. At Grantsville, Franklin W. was married to Nancy Green, and in September, 1859, he received a call from President Brigham Young to come to Salt Lake City, prepared to go on a mission. Dropping everything, he hastened to the city, where on September 14, 1859, he was ordained a bishop and set apart to preside over Payson. He was twenty years, six months, and twenty-seven days old. The ward at Payson at that time had about 175 families, besides a branch at Pondtown, now Salem, of about twenty-five families. For two years the "Boy Bishop," as he was often called, struggled in the midst of the Saints of his ward, but when President Brigham Young saw that it was telling on the young man, and that he was trying to carry too great a load, he called him on a mission to the cotton country, or "Dixie," to help to build up the barren wastes there.[29]

NOTES

1. *History of the Church*, edited by B. H. Roberts (Salt Lake City: Deseret Book, 1950), 5:349–49.
2. Ibid.
3. M. Guy Bishop, "A Great Little Saint: A Brief Look at the Life of Henry William Bigler," *BYU Studies*, 30:4, 33.
4. Brandon S. Plewe, et. at., *Mapping Mormonism* (Provo, Utah: Brigham Young University Press, 2012), 163.
5. *History of the Saints,* Harley, William G., ed. (American Fork, Utah: Covenant Communications, 2012), 157.
6. Richard S. Van Wagoner and Steven C. Walker, *A Book of Mormons* (Salt Lake City: Signature Books, 1982), 50.
7. Eugene E. Campbell, "The Mormon Gold-Mining Mission of 1849," *BYU Studies,* Vol. 1, Issue 2, 1959, 29–30.
8. Eugene E. Campbell, "The Mormon Gold-Mining Mission of 1849," 29–30.
9. Ibid.
10. Leonard J. Arrington, *Great Basin Kingdom* (Cambridge: University Press, 1958); Eugene E. Campbell, "Mormon Gold Mining Mission of 1849." *BYU Studies* 2 (Winter 1960), 19–31, August 1959.
11. Arnold K. Garr et al., *Encyclopedia of Latter-day Saint History* (Salt Lake City: Deseret Book, 2000), 1142.
12. Ronald W. Walker and Doris R. Dant ed., *Nearly Everything Imaginable (*Provo, Utah: BYU Press, 1999), 377.
13. ivybridge-heritage.org/archive/the-use-of-rags-in-paper-making/
14. Monte Burr McLaws, *Spokesman for the Kingdom* (Provo, Utah: Brigham Young University Press, 1977), 30.
15. Monte Burr McLaws, *Spokesman for the Kingdom*, 30.

16. Judy Fraser, *Did You Know . . . Hidden Treasures from Church History* (Orem, Utah: Granite Publishers, 1996), 98.
17. Monte Burr McLaws, *Spokesman for the Kingdom* (Provo, Utah: Brigham Young University Press, 1977), 30.
18. Andrew Jenson, *LDS Biographical Encyclopedia* (Salt Lake City: Publishers Press, 1901) 1:332.
19. Ibid., 227.
20. Lesson Committee, Museum Memories-Daughters of Utah Pioneers (Salt Lake City, Talon Printing, 2010), 2:240.
21. Andrew Jenson, *LDS Biographical Encyclopedia* (Salt Lake City: Andrew Jenson History Company, 1914), 44.
22. Jerry H. Houck, *Witnesses of Christ: Prophets and Apostles of our Dispensation* (Cedar Fort: Springville, Utah, 2015), 222–23.
23. Andrew Jenson, *LDS Biographical Encyclopedia*, 98.
24. churchofjesuschrist.org/study/manual/revelations-in-context/leman-copley-and-the-shakers?lang=eng
25. Lawrence R. Flake, *Mighty Men of Zion* (Salt Lake City: Karl D. Butler, 1974), 237.
26. Leonard J. Arrington, "Religion and Economics in Mormon History," *BYU Studies*, Journal 3:3–4.
27. speeches.byu.edu/talks/jeffrey-r-holland/times-trouble/
28. Andrew Jenson, *LDS Biographical Encyclopedia* (Salt Lake City: Andrew Jenson History Company, 1914), 44.
29. Ibid., 97.

Mission Training

Today we're familiar with missionaries reporting to the Missionary Training Center in Provo, Utah, or any of the other MTCs located throughout the world. This was the current practice until, because of recent world events, the Church implemented necessary measures to protect their missionary force from COVID-19. As a result of the pandemic, MTCs were closed. Similar to those in primary and secondary education, missionaries trained at home for a period and then were sent to their missions. How things have changed just in my lifetime. When I was called (1977), I spent five days in the mission home across the street from the fairly new Church Office Building tower. This was the old Lafayette School that was converted into a mission home for all elders called to English-speaking countries. Those called to countries where they were required to learn a new language were sent to the Language Training Mission (LTM), currently the MTC in Provo. It was a short six months after I went through the mission home in Salt Lake City when it was closed, the building leveled, and a parking lot constructed in its place. From this point on, all missionaries were routed to Provo, Utah, or any one of a number of MTCs around the world. Nevertheless, up to this point in the book, we've learned that the Church has had numerous practices that no longer exist, the mission home experience included.

In 1900, the General Church Board of Education opened missionary training courses at Latter-day Saints Academy in Thatcher, Arizona, Brigham Young Academy in Provo, Brigham Young College in Logan, and the Latter-day Saint University in Salt Lake City. This wasn't for elders who had been called, but rather for perspective missionaries.[1] Prior to my mission, and currently in use by I imagine most stakes in the Church, I attended mission prep classes. These classes were on Sunday evenings, during which time we discussed gospel topics along with corresponding scriptures. In 1900, it wasn't this way. In fact, this was a six-month course, taught daily as if the perspective missionary were a regular student. This mission prep course may have been the only course on these schools campuses that taught tuition free. However, for those that had to leave home to take the course, the local stakes were instructed to provide board and lodging.[2]

NOTES

1. The Church of Jesus Christ of Latter-day Saints, *Church History In The Fulness Of Time* (Salt Lake City: Published by The Church of Jesus Christ of Latter-day Saints, 1993), 459.
2. Ibid.

Missionaries

Those called on missions today may not have a section in the Doctrine and Covenants specifically devoted to them with the Lord's instruction to them personally, similar to the situation of Orson Pratt and section 34. Nevertheless, what they do have is an inspired mission call from the prophet with the same invitation the Lord shared with Orson. Doctrine and Covenants 34:5 states, "And more blessed are you because *you are called to preach my gospel*."[1]

For much of the history of the Church, men of all ages were called to serve. It was not uncommon for sixteen-year-old young men to be summoned to serve and preach the gospel. It was also common for men with families to serve in all parts of the world spreading the gospel, while their wives and families supported them. I was somewhat amazed when my father, who served his mission in the mid-1950's, shared that he had a married companion. By time I served my mission in the late 1970s, married men no longer were permitted to serve unless they were serving with their wives, or they were older, like my grandfather, whose wife had passed on. What was normal during the years I served was to have a large percentage of missionaries in the nineteen to twenty-one year range with a scattering of those throughout their twenties to early thirties. When and who was the first to be called as a nineteen-year-old missionary after the Church standardized the age for missionaries? In June of 1960, Bruce R. McConkie set apart Joseph Fielding McConkie, his nineteen-year-old son, to serve as a missionary for the Church.[2]

For a few decades, the Church used sports and music to spread the gospel. For instance, future Apostle Marvin J. Ashton was part of an all-missionary basketball team that won the Great Britain national basketball championship on April 19, 1938.[3]

Australian mission president Charles Liljenquist had a vision (not literally) of using basketball as a tool for the spread of the gospel. In 1954 the Harlem Globetrotters toured the Australian continent, creating excitement for the game. President Liljenquist saw Adelaide as the city to unfold his experiment. He organized an elite team of players, one that included future General Authority Loren C. Dunn, turning them loose on the city. The team experienced instant success. It was not uncommon for the Australian Tennis Association to invite the basketball playing elders to put on exhibitions prior to professional tennis matches as a gimmick to attract visitors. The Mormon Yankees, as the team was dubbed, attracted up to 9,000 people to view this display of skill.[4]

During a tour of Australia, and while questioned by the press, President David O. McKay first learned of the Mormon Yankees. After the news conference the prophet approached the mission president and asked him to explain. Needless to say, the prophet was impressed by what he heard. President Liljenquist lamented the fact that when Elder Dunn and the other ball players completed their missions the program would fold. President McKay encouraged President Liljenquist to keep the team intact and he would do what he could from his end to send talented basketball players to his mission. President McKay didn't disappoint. He sent such college stars as Bob Skousen, DeLyle Condie, Mark Frodsham, and Don Hull to serve two-year missions in Australia. It was the Mormon Yankees that helped train the Australian National Basketball team to prepare for the Olympics. While training the Australians, the Mormon Yankees defeated other Olympic teams, countries such as France, Chile, Taiwan, and Australia, only losing by nine points to the eventual silver medalist, Russians.[5]

Then things escalated. In 1957, the players on the team convinced their mission president to send them to outlying areas around the country to open areas where missionaries had not previously served, or towns where playing a game against the local squad could help promote missionary work in the area. The team gained the sponsorship of Volkswagen of Australia, which included a van and publicity. This led to clinics for the youth along with firesides, leading to intensified efforts in proselyting.[6]

The end came in 1961 when Church authorities announced that the Church no longer encouraged elders to use sports as a means to spread the gospel. The Australians were devastated, when some disappointed residents approached local Church leaders asking for a reversal in the decision. The Church held firm with their verdict.[7] It's noteworthy that even though using sports as a way to generate awareness in the Church was officially nixed, in 1967 the idea resurfaced in Italy. This had minimal success, and at the end of the first season the team disbanded.[8]

The same was true for South Africa. During the 1920s and into the early 1930s, the Church was failing at favorable press. Mission president Don Mack Dalton believed by forming a baseball team he could turn the tide of popularity in favor of the Church's image. In 1931, the Cumorah Baseball Club, or the Cumorah's, as they were affectionately called, was formed. To be honest, South Africa was not the first mission to experiment with baseball. As surprising as it may seem, one missionary participated on a religious mix of players in 1911 in Japan. An all-missionary team composed of elders from The Church of Jesus Christ of Latter-day Saints played in Samoa in 1923–24 in hopes of developing good relationships with the locals. In 1935, the *Millennial Star* in Britain was contacted by Harry Holland. The purpose of the contact was to invite missionaries from the Church to field a baseball team in the eight-team National Baseball Association. The elders in the area consented and appropriately christened themselves the "Latter-day Saints."

Elder Wendell (Buzz) Ashton, a member of the team recounted: "To the Church, baseball in Britain is proving a powerful instrument for breaking down barriers of prejudice that existed for nearly a century and for opening the way (for Britons) to hear the Gospel message. . . . Scores of people in Great Britain are learning through baseball that Mormon means more good."[9]

Few baptisms were generated, so one could argue the fact that missionaries playing baseball might not be the best use of their time. If viewed that the public image of the Church improved, then the program was debatably successful. I can completely understand this. For whatever reason, sports has a way of soothing attitudes favorable to the gospel. I remember on occasion my companion and I on P-days enjoyed a little one-on-one at a local park in Portsmouth, New Hampshire. It was on one such occasion that a few locals saw us and immediately sent derogatory epithets our way. We ignored. However, they were relentless. Finally my companion asked them if they wanted to play two-on-two. My companion saw an opportunity to gain friends. What they saw were two guys that they thought they could bury. They accepted the challenge, and a few games later, after we defeated them, we had friends. They invited us to play ball with them anytime we wanted. We didn't baptize or even teach them. What we did do was diffuse a situation and gained respect.

So, back to the South African experiment. First off, why Cumorah as a team name? It's interesting that at the organization of the team, not just members of the Church were in attendance. It was said on August 10, 1932, attendees included "several business men, two doctors, a lawyer, an undertaker, some students, a Bible student missionary (and later convert), an atheist, some railway men, some members of the Church, and five missionaries." One elder suggested that since they were organizing in the Cumorah church in Cape Town that an appropriate name would be the Cumorah's.[10]

The Cumorah's were successful their first season. They did well enough that they found themselves contending in a best of five series for the Henry Hermann Cup in the Western Province Baseball Championship. The final series was played during the last week of January and the first two weeks of February in 1933. With the series tied, and the scored tied in the fifth and deciding game, mission president Dalton Mack states that the next batter up was the ninth and the one individual who struggled at bat. He was nicknamed the Suit Rack, in large part because his uniform hung on him. The Suit Rack, before exiting the dugout for the batting box, asked missionary/baseball player Don Dalton to pray for him. Dalton stated, "Pray for you! Yes, but I'm tired of praying for you! Go out there and hit that ball." The player rose to the occasion and shocked all when he knocked in the winning run.[11]

The success of this season caused President Dalton to write the following to his uncle, George Albert Smith: "Would it be possible for you to help get some more Elders down here of those kind who are good ball players, a good pitcher is badly needed—that is if you approve of my activity in baseball."[12] There is no record whether George Albert Smith approved of his mission president nephew's activity in baseball. However, if he didn't, Elder Richard R. Lyman was more than willing to do his part by sending talented elders his way. This would lead to twenty years of elders/baseball players called to serve in the South African Mission. The Church was instrumental for the growing popularity of the sport, so popular that people preferred it to rugby, cricket, and soccer. Just how popular did the South African baseball team become? They were so endeared by the public and the press that they received more press than the visit of Prince George to Capetown in 1935. What also didn't hurt was the arrival of Elder Stan Smith, a left-handed pitcher. It was said of him: "He has, no doubt, done more to shake the cold unfriendly barriers of distrust and skepticism concerning the Mormons there than any other person, for through his baseball he has moved with ease among the higher social circle and government officials. But more than all of this, he is the friend of more young people, staunch admirers, than another lad in South Africa."[13]

Through baseball, walls were dismantled. No longer did the general populace, when speaking of The Church of Jesus Christ of Latter-day Saints, point to polygamy and emigration. This was proven time and time again in the press, including books. It was about this time that Eric Rosenthal, feeling the importance to educate people about South Africa due to the increasing tourist industry, included a chapter on the Church. This wouldn't have happened if it wasn't for baseball and the Cumorah's. The following is one such example of a newspaper article:

> Baseball players in the Western Province Leagues, and sportsmen as a whole, will rally to hear Stan Smith, the outstanding baseball pitcher, speak. Stan left his home in Salt Lake City some time ago as a Mormon missionary. For diversion and to keep physically fit he began playing baseball and his pitching brought honors. Being young and possessing outstanding athletic ability, Stan has achieved a wonderful degree of popularity which is well deserved. He has consented to lecture for us on Religious Ideals at the Railway Institute on Saturday evening at 8 o'clock. If Stan is as convincing from the platform as he is from the pitcher's box his success is assured.[14]

However, the respect was not in the newspapers alone but also on the field of play. An all-star team was assembled from players from the various teams in the Western Province League. Five players, and all missionaries, were players from the Cumorah's. Those invited to play in the game were Don Mack Dalton, the mission president who had the idea to organize the team as well as play on it (he also had a mean bat), as well as Elders Stanford G. Smith, John J. Bates, Morris P. Woolley, and E. E. Seeman, a local member. On game day, as the pre-game ceremonies were in progress, George Herbert Hyde Villiers, the sixth earl of Clarendon, shook all the hands of the players as they stood in line. It was the privilege and honor of President Dalton to introduce the players on his team to the earl. When the earl shook each missionary's hand, he referred to each one as "Elder." Yes, The Church of Jesus Christ of Latter-day Saints had gained respect. Part of this respect was in the attendance of home games where usually 800 spectators enjoyed their games. The all-star game didn't disappoint either, with 2,500 fans in attendance.[15]

It's interesting that prior to 1935, the mission was accustomed to approximately eight or nine new elders sent to the South African Mission. With the Cumorah's championship season, many new elders were called to serve in South Africa. Between 1935 to 1940, 158 new missionaries were called. This increase was enough to form another missionary baseball team, the Nauvoo Legion, in Port Elizabeth. This team lasted a year due to two of the best players being transferred to other areas of South Africa. A third team of either elders, or one-time elders who returned to South Africa as businessmen in an ice cream store chain, was formed in 1936, known as the Johannesburg Americans.[16]

There is no way this would fly today. Missionaries are viewed as those worthy to spread the gospel through meeting and teaching people on the streets and in their homes, not on basketball courts or baseball diamonds.

• • •

It's remarkable that prior to February 4, 1902, missionaries were required to pay tithing on money earned. Prior to this date, it was not uncommon for missionaries to work to earn their way. Where I typically read about this type of practice are missionaries who were called to Europe or the Sandwich and other south Pacific Islands. Elders traveled without purse or scrip, relying on the goodness of others for food and money to meet their needs. Sometimes the Saints were generous enough for a missionary to provide for his passage without seeking employment. However, in some cases, the Saints couldn't always provide, and this is when the missionary gained employment and raised money. Because of this, tithing would have been paid. Today's missionaries devote 100 percent of their time in the Lord's service. The money to provide for the missionaries needs comes from what the elder saved prior to his mission, his family, ward, or through Church donations. Because of this, there is little reason to tithe.[17]

• • •

What happens when wars plague the earth and young men from various countries have an obligation to serve, not missions, but take up arms for their nations, who then serves? It's interesting that during World War I in Britain the local sisters took the responsibility of missionary work on their shoulders.[18]

The following from the experience of Henry Eyring's mission to the Cherokee:

> In May, 1860, after having labored in the Indian Territory four and a half years, I started for Utah, where I arrived Aug. 29, 1860. At that time the Cherokee Mission was under the direct charge of the Presidency in Utah, but it was very difficult in those days to get any news from there. I had had charge of the mission for over two years, and altogether had been in that field nearly four and a half years; hence I began to think that possibly my mission might come to a close before long. Getting no news of an kind from Utah, I inquired of the Lord and He answered me in a dream, as follows: I dreamed that I was in the President's office in Salt Lake City, and that I addressed Pres. Young, saying: "I have come of my own accord, but if I have not stayed long enough, I am willing to return and complete my mission." The president answered: "It is all right, you have stayed long enough." On the strength of this dream I started for Utah; and when I met the President, I said to him: "Pres. Young, I have come without being sent for; if this was not right, I am willing to go back and finish my mission." He answered pleasantly: "It is all right, we have been looking for you."[19]

• • •

In February 1833, Joseph Smith received the revelation know as section 89, the Word of Wisdom. It was many years after this revelation, even decades, when the Word of Wisdom became a temple worthiness requirement. For many years after the revelation was received, not all members of the Church adhered to its principles. Members smoked and continued to drink alcoholic beverages in Nauvoo and the Salt Lake Valley. This was also true of the missionaries who were sent on missions. Some missionaries also drank on occasion. During the 1839 mission to Britain it was not uncommon for missionaries to drink an occasional glass of wine or beer with their meals. Wilford Woodruff and Heber C. Kimball, while in Britain in 1841, toured the largest wine vault in the world and participated in tasting the wine at the end of the tour, stating, "Found the wine a good article."[20]

• • •

Tracting is a practice that is fading as a way to conduct missionary work. While I was on my mission, an area achieved superior recognition if one of the requirements met was twenty-five hours tracting through the course of the week. While serving in my last area I ran into an individual from Scotland who felt the North American missions were getting off light, since in his country it was common for elders to tract up to sixty hours a week. Obviously a difference in local laws. We weren't permitted to tract after five o'clock in the afternoon. For those missionaries serving during the 1800s, tracting wasn't practiced the way it was on my mission. It was more common for elders to set meetings in halls or at people's homes and then advertise. Usually these meetings were well attended, whether or not the intentions of those attending were sincere. However, the early missionaries would go from door to door and while doing so would try to sell the Book of Mormon and tracts. This is where the term "tracting" originates. While serving on my mission, I do recall selling a Book of Mormon or two (we generally gave them away). However, it never crossed my mind to sell tracts (pamphlets). We just didn't do this. Also, my companion and I never split while tracting. We stayed together from door to door throughout the day. This wasn't the case during the 1800s. It was typical for the companionship to divide. While one companion tract one side of the street, the other companion tract the other side.[21]

NOTES

1. churchofjesuschrist.org/study/manual/revelations-in-context/orson-pratts-call-to-serve?lang=eng
2. Richard Neitzel Holzapfel, et al., *On This Day In The Church* (Salt Lake City: Eagle Gate, 2000), 129.
3. Richard Neitzel Holzapfel et. Al., *On This Day in the Church,* 77.
4. Fred E. Woods, "Mormon Yankees: Giant son and off the Court," *BYU Studies*, Vol. 53, Number 1, 2014.
5. Ibid., 95–115.
6. Ibid.

7. Ibid.
8. James A. Toronto, The "Wild West of Missionary Work," Reopening the Italian Mission, 1965–71, *Journal of Mormon History*, Fall 2014, 44–45.
9. Fred E. Woods, "Mormon Yankees: Giant son and off the Court," 95–115.
10. Ibid.
11. Ibid.
12. Ibid.
13. Ibid.
14. Ibid.
15. Ibid.
16. Ibid.
17. Richard Neitzel Holzapfel, et al., *On This Day In The Church* (Salt Lake City: Eagle Gate, 2000), 26.
18. V. Ben Bloxham, James R. Moss, and Larry C. Porter, eds. *Truth Will Prevail: The Rise of The Church of Jesus Christ of Latter-day Saints in the British Isles, 1837–1997* (Cambridge: Cambridge University Press, 1987).
19. Andrew Jenson, *LDS Biographical Encyclopedia* (Salt Lake City: Publishers Press, 1901) 1:312–313.
20. James B. Allen, et. al, *Men with a Mission 1937–1841*, (Salt Lake City: Deseret Book, 1992), 103–104.
21. Rebecca Bartholomew, *Audacious Women—Early British Mormon Immigrants* (Salt Lake City: Signature Books, 1995), 57–58.)

Money

In the 1970s I had an older cousin who purchased a bar of silver. He stored the bar in a cloth sack, and being curious I asked if I could see it. To me it was an interesting sight, but more interesting was the false notion that I had a very wealthy cousin. What I didn't understand is that the bar was valued less than when he originally purchased it. Little did I understand at the time the fluctuation in silver and gold created by situations around the world and how these conditions affected the economy and prices of commodities such as metals. Prior to his purchase, silver took off, rising very fast in value. My cousin jumped on the bandwagon, but he jumped on too late. Shortly after his purchase the price of silver dropped.

When the Saints first settled in the Salt Lake Valley, money was scarce. It's interesting that a number of Saints still had in their possession worthless cash in the form of leftover bills from the Kirtland Safety Society Anti-banking institution failure. Those still clinging to these valueless notes may have seen it as a souvenir, a reminder of their Kirtland years, or similar to my cousin, some were clinging to the hope that one day it would actually be worth something.

Then the miracle materialized. I'm sure when Brigham Young viewed the valley for the first time and proclaimed, "This is the place, move on," he envisioned the Saints safely tucked away in this desert region for years, or maybe decades, out of the reach of those who would do them harm. True, the only occupants were the Saints and the natives, but it wasn't this way for decades, or even years. Rather, two short years later an estimated 10,000 gold seekers cut through Salt Lake City on their trek to the California gold fields.

Things were definitely lean. To state that life was difficult in the valley those first two years was a clear understatement. It hardly seemed long ago when Heber C. Kimball astonished the Saints, and even himself, when he prophesied that cloth on the streets of Salt Lake City would be purchased cheaper than in the eastern cities. How could that be? The Saints couldn't buy cloth if they wanted to. They could barter with the few crops that they did produce, but to buy with money was out of the question simply because there was very little. Nevertheless, the miracle came in the form of the 10,000 fortune seekers tromping through the Saints' valley. Many accounts tell of the gold seekers who, wanting to hit the gold fields faster, unloaded commodities to the Saints at a fraction of the price. True, these exchanges weren't in the form of monetary transactions, but rather the Saints bartering what little they had in the form of commodities to gain better and more commodities. I'm sure as each transaction materialized, the Saints realized that Heber actually knew what he was talking about.[1]

It wasn't long after this when the Mormon Battalion soldiers reunited with their families in the valley, bringing with them a ready supply of gold dust, much of which found a safe haven in the coffers of the Church. On March 9, 1849, the First Presidency issued the following epistle:

> On the return of a portion of the Mormon Battalion through the northern part of Western California, they discovered an extensive gold mine which enable them by a few days delay to bring sufficient of the dust to make money plentiful in this place for all ordinary convenience; in the exchange the brethren deposited the gold dust with the presidency, who issued bills of paper currency.
>
> Owing to the wonderful appeal that free gold makes to the imagination, it is easily possible to exaggerate the size of the piles brought to Deseret from the coast. The most definite information relative to the amount of this commodity handled by Brigham Young is contained in a business memorandum of his daily transactions in gold dust from December 10, 1848 to October 8, 1849, a ten-month interval, which discloses that he received in exchange for notes, American Coin and Valley Coin, gold dust to the value of at least $10,968.04.[2]

Those who tossed their paper currency at the time of the Kirtland Safety Society failure, who used it to start their evening fire, may have been feeling a little more than foolish at the rash decision to rid themselves of a bad memory. Those still clinging to their money, with the hope of reclaiming their losses, were blessed in this endeavor. With the gold dust as backing, the Church was able to reissue the Kirtland bank notes. However, Brigham didn't stop here. He instituted a mint in Salt Lake City and appointed John Kay to manufacture gold coins in denominations of ten dollars, twenty dollars, sixty dollars, and smaller amounts. This was designated as Valley Coin and Deseret Coin.[3] If you were fortunate enough to hold one of these coins today, like I felt privileged to hold my cousin's silver bar, what would it look like? These coins were minted with the "all seeing eye" on one side and on the flip side the words "Holiness to the Lord" spelled out in the new Deseret alphabet.[4]

Today the Saints no longer use the money minted by the Church but rather transact business, pay tithing, save, and flip a coin to see who goes first with the same money that all Americans of all faiths use—that issued by the Federal Treasury. Similar to the Deseret and Valley Coin, this too has an insignia. It might not be the words that are strictly unique to those belonging to this Church. Nevertheless, it has a message that touches the hearts of all Christian people: "In God We Trust."

Another point of interest, and a rule that no longer exists today, was a proclamation by Brigham Young, essentially declaring that it was against Church protocol for any man to hoard property or money. President Young stated the following:

> When we first came into the Valley, the question was asked me, if men would ever be allowed to come into this Church, and remain in it, and hoard up their property. I say NO. . . . The man who lays up his gold and silver, who caches it away in a bank or in his iron safe, or buries it up in the earth and comes here, and professes to be a Saint, would tie up the hands of every individual in this kingdom, and make them his servants if he could. It is an unrighteous, unhallowed, unholy, covetous principle; it is of the devil and is from beneath . . . *"would disfellowship a man who had received liberally from the Lord, a refused to put it out to usury."*
>
> "You know very well," he concluded, "that it is against church doctrine for men to scrape together the wealth of the world and let it waste and do not good."[5]

I'm sure the Church would like those that are in a position to do so to do good with their money. Trust me, there are many wealthy members of The Church of Jesus Christ of Latter-day Saints who do this. There are countless Saints possessing the understanding that they have been blessed richly by the Lord and give back to the Church and community. Temples have been raised, hospitals and universities have been constructed, and many millions of dollars have been donated to worthy charities from the pockets of Saints understanding the true meaning of wealth. So really, this isn't any different from the days of Brigham Young, except in the current size of donations as opposed to the contributions in the Utah pioneer Church. What has changed from Brigham Young's statement over a century ago, though, is the notion of not placing money in a safe or a bank. Believe it or not, I had an uncle who buried his money. This, too, Brigham didn't care for. However, to be fair to my uncle, he experienced the Great Depression. He was present when my grandfather received back from the bank one dollar for every ten that he had deposited. So, is it any wonder my uncle would bury his money? That he would distrust the current financial system established in this country? No, I don't blame him at all. However, at conference time, do we hear our leaders encouraging us to save for a rainy day? Yes, I'm sure they would like to see all members of the Church save for unforeseen circumstances and be self-sufficient enough to survive a temporary setback or emergency.

NOTES

1. *Chronicles of Courage,* Lesson Committee (Salt Lake City: Talon Printing, 1996), Vol. 7, 65–67.
2. Ibid.
3. *History of the Saints,* Harley, William G., ed. (American Fork, Utah: Covenant Communications, 2012), 171.
4. Lawrence R. Flake, Prophets and Apostles of the Last Dispensation (Provo, Utah: Religious Study Center, Brigham Young University, 2001), 372–373; Kathryn Jenkins Gordon, *Colorful Characters in Mormon History* (American Fork, Utah: Covenant Communications Inc., 2015), 137–38; byui.edu/special-collections/deseret-alphabet; *Chronicles of Courage,* Lesson Committee (Salt Lake City: Talon Printing, 1996) Vol. 7, 65–67.
5. Leonard J. Arrington, "Religion and Economics in Mormon History," 24.

Newspapers—The Deseret News

Why would I include the *Deseret News* as a change in the Church? This newspaper existed in pioneer times (first published in June 1850) the way it does today.[1] Not much has changed. The change isn't in the fact that the Church has always had a newspaper, or more than one, in any given town or city during its history, but rather how the newspaper was used. Today the *Deseret News* provides people in the Salt Lake area and through the state with global, national, regional, and local news. I'm sure you might raise an eyebrow or two if I told you that missionaries during Territorial Utah learned of their mission releases in the field, calls to new missions, and on at least one occasion, a call to a new mission before being released from the mission they were currently serving in, in the columns of the *Deseret News.* For instance, in 1870, the *News* asked that Elder Samuel Savery return home immediately from his mission in the state of New York, since he wasn't in the "proper condition of mind."[2] Again, in 1877, Elder David King Udall learned by reading the *Deseret News,* while serving in England, that he was now called to a new mission in Arizona. Elder Udall said the following about the situation: "I am willing to respond but it seems strange that I am called to fill another mission before I am released from this one."[3]

It was also not uncommon during the pioneer Utah Church for the *Deseret News* to answer theological questions of its subscribers. As an example, subscriber Andrew Silver queried the *Deseret News* what caused the banishment of Satan from God. Using humor, Elder Parley P. Pratt answered: "I either was not present at the banishment of Satan, or have forgotten the particulars. The probability is, that he wished to go to a warmer climate for his health." To this the editor added, "Quite possibly he searched so deeply after the 'mysteries' of the kingdom, that he neglected his duties as many do at the present day."[4]

Rather than sending numerous letters to stake presidents and bishops, the leaders of the Church saw the *Deseret News* as a means to communicate what was on their minds and what they wanted the local leaders to pass along to their membership. Such was the case during the Gold Rush. It was not uncommon for articles appearing in the *News* to the bishops discouraging the members of their wards dashing off to the gold fields of California. To help back the General Authorities, the paper printed articles on the down side to the Gold Rush, centering their arguments on the many thousands of men who gained nothing by making the trek for gold only to find nothing or spend what little they did find on the high cost of living.[5]

NOTES

1. Richard Neitzel Holzapfel, et al., *On This Day In The Church* (Salt Lake City: Eagle Gate, 2000), 118.
2. Monte Burr McLaws,*Spokesman for the Kingdom* (Provo, Utah: Brigham Young University Press, 1977), 59.
3. Ibid.
4. Ibid.
5. Ibid., 61–62.

Newspapers—The Mormon

During the mid-nineteenth century, the Church established several newspapers in eastern cities of the United States to combat the false impressions and reports made by mainstream newspapers of the day. In 1855, the Church, due to "bad" press, established a newspaper, *The Mormon*, in New York City. There was too much maliciousness by the other New York papers, and so to combat this the Church felt it beneficial to have its own paper rather than relying on the false claims and reports of others. To be clear, this need has failed to exist in the Church for quite some time. For the most part, the Saints are respected and rarely is the Church slandered and misrepresented the way it was in the 1800s. John Taylor was appointed editor and immediately went to work going toe to toe with any of the popular newspapers of the day in New York City.[1] Elder Taylor was never shy in the language he used in his defense or attacks. The following is a brief example: "Your malicious slanders only excite contempt for those base enough to utter them. . . . Talk to us with your hypocritical cant. . . . Pshaw! It's nauseating to everyone not eaten up with your corrupt humbuggery and pharisaical egotism."[2]

NOTES

1. Monte Burr McLaws, *Spokesman for the Kingdom* (Provo, Utah: Brigham Young University Press, 1977), 72–73.
2. Monte Burr McLaws, *Spokesman for the Kingdom*, 72–73.

Patriarchal Blessings

On December 9, 1834, shortly after his call as the patriarch to the Church, Joseph Smith Sr. laid his hands on the head of his Prophet son, Joseph Jr. and stated: "Joseph, my son, I lay my hands upon thy head in the name of the Lord Jesus Christ, to confirm upon thee a father's blessing. The Lord thy God has called thee by name out of the heavens: thou hast heard his voice from on high from time to time, even in thy youth."[1]

Since this time, and continuing through to 1979, the Church has had a patriarch at the head of the Church. In 1979 the Church patriarch, Eldredge G. Smith, was given emeritus status. This action took place due to the number of local patriarchs called in the stakes of Zion throughout the world.[2]

At the bishop's discretion, young people can obtain a recommend to visit their stake patriarch and, under the hands of the patriarch, receive a patriarchal blessing. Currently, we qualify for one blessing at the hands of a patriarch. This is the blessing we are given for this life. My mom was disappointed with her blessing, not in its contents but rather its length. True, it was shorter than most. However, the patriarch that provided the blessing nailed her life on the head. He couldn't have been more accurate as every promise was fulfilled in a beautiful way. She couldn't have seen it at the time she received it. However, as her life came to a close, she knew that she was given a very special blessing.

This isn't the way it's always been. In fact, from the autobiography of Lorenzo Hill Hatch we learn that he received four patriarchal blessings and that his wife, Sylvia, was blessed with two.[3] Angus Cannon was another individual who received four blessings over his lifetime under the hands of John Smith in 1853 and a second one in 1867, a third blessing from William G. Perkins in 1874, and finally in 1886 from Zebedee Coltrin.[4]

As odd as it may seem, even non-members received patriarchal blessings in the early pioneer Church. Thomas L. Kane, friend of the Saints but not a member himself, appears to have received two. His wife, Elizabeth, also not a member of the Church, received a blessing in 1873 and later recorded the following: "The blessing was somewhat prophetical, and so far as it was did not coincide with one given K. long ago by the old patriarch John Smith, which has been curiously fulfilled so far, strange to say."[5]

It's remarkable that a number of Saints, like Sarah Dugard, received a blessing in both Nauvoo and Salt Lake City.[6] Similar to those who were rebaptized when they entered the valley, they might have also felt the need for a new patriarchal blessing as an outward sign and commitment to their faith.

An additional difference in the early Church, and carrying through to the Utah Territorial years, is that patriarchs were paid for their services. The following from the *History of the Church:*

> September 14, 1835—In a meeting of a High Council and the Presidency at Kirtland, it was decided that, as the laborer is worthy of his hire, whenever president Joseph Smith, Sen., is called upon to pronounce Patriarchal blessings upon the Church, he be paid for his services at the rate of ten dollars per week and his expenses. It was further decided that President Frederick G. Williams be appointed and hereafter serve as scribe, to attend blessing meetings, and that he receive for his services, at the same ratio, having his expenses borne also.
>
> December 6, 1837—Voted that the recorder of licenses and patriarchal blessings receive, for each one hundred words, ten cents.[7]

Again, the following:

> November 30, 1837—It is our united opinion that the Presidency, High Council, Bishop and counselors, clerk of the council, Patriarch and agents of the Church (also any others who may be employed in Church business), receive per day, each, one dollar and fifty cents.
>
> Simeon Carter,
> Elias Higbee,
> Elisha G. Groves[8]

Patriarch, Angus M. Cannon records the following, "Gave 7 Patriarchal blessings for which each gave $1. . . . Ann wrote them for me and I gave Ann $3.00 for writing them for us."[9]

Today we hear people state that their patriarchal blessing is too sacred to share. In fact, we have been counseled to be cautious what we share when it comes to these special blessings. These blessings are specific to that individual and never should a person be asked to read or share their blessing, unless the individual voluntarily shares.[10] This isn't always the way it's been through history. In fact, patriarchal blessings used to be given during blessing meetings for all who attended to enjoy.[11]

It also wasn't unusual for husbands and wives during the Nauvoo years of the Church to receive their blessing collectively. It is said that Hyrum Smith, when ordaining men to priesthood offices, also took the pleasure of providing them with a patriarchal blessing, even if they had already received one. It was also in Nauvoo when people received a blessing first from Joseph Smith Sr. and then an additional blessing from William Smith, Joseph Sr.'s son.[12]

It's remarkable that William Smith provided blessings for two deceased women by proxy. When William inquired if this was a correct principle, Brigham told him that "it is not according to the order of the church to confer Patriarchal Blessings on the dead by proxy, until baptism has been attended to for them by proxy, which must be done in the Lord's House."[13]

During the early years of the Church, Joseph Smith Sr. provided a patriarchal blessing to David Whitmer, without David actually being present for the blessing.[14]

Matthew Cowley received his blessing as a six-year-old.[15] This seems a little young, at least to us today. The teenage years have become the current norm. Nevertheless, the fact that Brother Cowley received it so young in life in no way deterred from what was in store for him. His blessing read, "You shall be sent as a delegate to the ten tribes and will become a leader and an interpreter in the midst of that people, and because of the power of God that shall be without and the blessings of the Almighty, you shall be greatly beloved by that people."[16]

As a seventeen-year-old missionary, Elder Cowley was called to serve among the Maoris of New Zealand. This would be a five-year mission, during which time he translated the Pearl of Great Price and the Doctrine and Covenants. He also edited the Book of Mormon, which had previously been translated.[17]

NOTES

1. josephsmithpapers.org/paper-summary/blessing-from-joseph-smith-sr-9–december-1834/1
2. history.churchofjesuschrist.org/blog/a-history-of-patriarchs-and-patriarchal-blessings?lang=eng
3. *Autobiography of Lorenzo Hill Hatch*, Typescript, Harold B. Lee Library, Brigham Young University.
4. Donald Q. Cannon and David J. Whittaker, *Supporting Saints: Life Stories of Nineteenth-Century Mormons* (Salt Lake City: Bookcraft Inc., 1985), 387.
5. David J. Whittaker, "My Dear Friend," *BYU Studies,* Volume 48, Number 4, 2009, 201; Elizabeth Kane, St. George Journal, February 11, 1873, Kane Collection, Perry Special Collections, Harold B. Lee Library, Brigham Young University.

6. Ronald W. Walker and Doris R. Dant ed., *Nearly Everything Imaginable* (Provo, Utah: BYU Press, 1999), 273.
7. *History of the Church* 2:273, 528.
8. *History of the Church* 2:527.
9. Donald Q. Cannon and David J. Whittaker, *Supporting Saints: Life Stories of Nineteenth-Century Mormons* (Salt Lake City: Bookcraft Inc., 1985), 387–388.
10. history.churchofjesuschrist.org/blog/a-history-of-patriarchs-and-patriarchal-blessings?lang=eng
11. Marquardt, H. Michael, *Early Patriarchal Blessings of The Church of Jesus Christ of Latter-day Saints* (Salt Lake City: The Smith-Pettit Foundation, 2007), vii.
12. Marquardt, H. Michael, *Early Patriarchal Blessings of The Church of Jesus Christ of Latter-day Saints* (Salt Lake City: The Smith-Pettit Foundation, 2007), xi.
13. Ibid., xv.
14. Ibid., 49.
15. Lawrence R. Flake, *Prophets and Apostles of the Last Dispensation* (Provo, Utah: Religious Study Center, Brigham Young University, 2001), 481–482.
16. Ibid.
17. Ibid.

Politics

Have you ever wondered how a political system would work in a society composed of a singular religion in an area, where others of various denominations were hundreds of miles distant? Really, not that big of a deal. At least this was the thought of the Saints. It made sense for Church heads to choose political leaders and then organize an election where the names were presented and those in attendance would raise their arms to the square to ratify the choice. One such incident took place when the Council of Fifty, on March 4, 1849, chose Brigham Young as governor, Willard Richards as secretary of state, Heber C. Kimball as chief justice, Joseph K. Heywood as supervisor of roads, Newel K. Whitney as treasurer, Newel K. Whitney and John Taylor as associate judges,

Horace S. Eldredge as marshal, Albert Carrington as assessor and collector, and Daniel H. Wells as attorney general. On March 12, 1849 the election was held for positions in the provisional state of Deseret when 674 people raised their arm to the square in favor, with none opposed. This was the practice up until Utah became a territory (September 1850), in which case Brigham Young was appointed by the President of the United States to serve as governor.

Only in Utah![1]

NOTES

1. Peter Crawley, "The Constitution of the State of Deseret." *BYU Studies,* Fall 1989, 10.

Prayer

Prayer, as we know it, is a powerful tool that allows us to communicate to our Heavenly Father. If used with humility and with faith, it can be a source of strength to us during times of trials and times of abundant blessings. When I first entered the mission field I was certain I had entered with a testimony of the gospel. It didn't take long for me to realize that what I thought was my personal testimony was in truth me leaning on the testimony of my parents. It boiled down to the fact that they told me the gospel was true and I believed it. There was nothing wrong with this, I suppose, other than the testimony was borrowed; it wasn't mine. I trusted my parents and knew they would never lead me astray on spiritual matters. I determined if I was going to be successful in the field, then it was imperative that I gain my own testimony of the gospel. I remember the afternoon well when I hit the crossroads of either sharing what someone else knew to be true as opposed to what I knew was correct. I knelt down in our trailer house that my companion and I lived in between the towns of Guilford and Sangerville, Maine. I was earnest for an answer. It was the first time in my life that I approached Heavenly Father with a burning desire to know the truth. I wasn't on my knees but a short time when what the scriptures refer to as "a burning of the bosom" enveloped my entire body. It was an incredible sensation that lingered and left me knowing that what I was telling the people of New England was the truth, and could continue my mission in confidence. Nevertheless, this isn't just me. Millions of Saints who have lived or are currently living have accessed the same source through prayer and have received the inspiration necessary to go on. As it is, this dispensation opened with a humble prayer.

I have sat in numerous meetings from seminary to family home evening and family scripture study to general conference and have heard from my teachers, parents, and spiritual leaders how to unlock the heavens through prayer. Zina Diantha Young shares with the sisters in her area what she felt was an aid, that if used, could help answers inquiries to our Heavenly Father. At a meeting held on February 14, 1895, Zina Diantha Young instructed the women to kneel with their faces toward the temple. Her reasoning? Because "President Wilford Woodruff had promised the Saints when they desired any special blessing from the Lord if they should do so, it would be granted to them."[1]

I'm beating a dead horse when I mention for the umpteenth time this book is about change. It's a study of what we used to practice in the Church compared to the way we exercise the same principle today. Much of this book points to change at a Church level. However, I share some modifications that may have only been used or practiced in a few wards or stakes. What I just shared is change in a more personal, individual situation. There may still be families who pray facing the temple, particularly those with a temple in the near vicinity, but for the most part, I think many of us give it little thought.

NOTE

1. Martha Sonntag Bradley and Mary Brown Firmage Woodward, *4 Zinas* (Signature Books: Salt Lake City, 2000)

Prayer Circles (Outside of the Temple)

If you're endowed, you're familiar with prayer circles in the temple. However, there was a time when this was practiced in different individuals' homes during the Nauvoo years and in the meetinghouses in Territorial Utah. The prayer circle that Joseph Smith commenced in 1842 was referred to as the "Quorum," the "First Quorum," the "Quorum of the Anointed," or the "Holy Order." An initiation was required to gain membership. This initiation was in the form of a person receiving their washing and anointings. The group was limited in size, topping out at sixty-five members.[1]

Prayer circles continued for many years in individual homes, when in 1929, the First Presidency ended the exclusiveness of the practice, stating that the prayer circle outside the temple was not available to all worthy Church members and from this time forward would only be recognized within the walls of the temple.[2]

NOTES

1. James B. Allen, One Man's Nauvoo: William Clayton's Experience in Mormon Illinois, *Journal of Mormon History,* 1979, Vol. 6, Issue 1, 47.
2. Hugh Nibley, "The Early Christian Prayer Circle." BYU Studies 19 (Fall 1978), 41–78; Michael D. Quinn, "Latter-day Saint Prayer Circles." BYU Studies 19 (Fall 1978), 79–105.

Priesthood

The age at which an individual received the various offices in the priesthood has an interesting and unique history dating back to the organization of the Church. Today, we're accustomed to some young men becoming deacons at age eleven, teachers at thirteen, priests at fifteen, and elders at eighteen. However, it wasn't always this structured. For instance, many adult men in the early Church, 1829–45 held much of the Aaronic Priesthood offices, and yet, at the same time, many younger men, or men of Aaronic Priesthood age, were called to be elders or seventies and sent on missions. As odd as it may seem, Anthony Ivins, a future apostle of the Church, was ordained an elder at age thirteen. This would explain why there were three priests in attendance during the organization of the Church at the first conference of the Church on June 9, 1830. They were Joseph Smith Sr., fifty-nine; Hyrum Smith, thirty; and Martin Harris, forty-seven. In fact, the average age of the Nauvoo priest quorum was twenty-nine.[1]

During the organization of the Church, previous to the Nauvoo years, adult men holding the Aaronic Priesthood did not belong to ward quorums. At the time, the major responsibility of men holding the Aaronic Priesthood was to visit the homes of the members. In *History of the Church,* Joseph Smith provides the following insight to the deacons' responsibility during the Nauvoo years of the Church: "Elder Richards and I attended the deacon's meeting. The deacons have become very efficient looking after the welfare of the Saints; every part of the city is watched with the strictest care, and whatever time of night the streets are traveled, at the corner of every block a deacon is found attending to his duty."[2]

There was a shift in the number of adult men holding the Melchizedek Priesthood from 1846–77. This was due to the fact that the temple endowment was established and men had to hold the Melchizedek Priesthood to be endowed. Young men of Aaronic Priesthood age continued not to be ordained during the pioneer era and up to the mid-Utah Territorial years of the Church. This wouldn't happen until 1877, when young men worthy to hold the priesthood were ordained to the various offices in the Aaronic Priesthood.

It wasn't until 1908 that the various age groups corresponding to the various Aaronic Priesthood offices began to be standardized. Deacons were ordained at twelve, teachers at fifteen, priests at eighteen, and elders at twenty-one. This was restructured again in 1928, when ages for the various offices were set at twelve, fifteen, seventeen, and elders at twenty. In 1954, the ages were set at twelve, fourteen, and sixteen, with elders at twenty.[3] Today, as of 2021, some young men are called to the office of deacon in the Aaronic Priesthood as early as eleven years of age and elders at eighteen.[4]

It was significant that when the Saints first arrived in Utah, and for a number of years later, that elders quorums and high priest groups were far and few between. However, to belong to the seventies quorum was far more common with sixty such quorums existing in Utah in the 1860s. This was due to the fact that many men called on missions were not always called as elders. More often than not, they were called as seventies. What's compelling about the seventy quorums is if a man was called to the Twenty-first Quorum of the Seventy, served a mission, came home, and then moved to another locality in the territory, he still belonged to the Twenty-first Quorum of the Seventy.[5]

Double duty in the priesthood was common during Brigham Young's presidency. It was also during this time period when one encountered the phrase "I was an elder before I was a deacon." To those holding the priesthood in those days, this phrase made perfect sense. For instance, a man might be an elder in the Melchizedek Priesthood but called as an acting deacon in the same ward or another ward other than his own. It was also not uncommon for men to hold the Melchizedek Priesthood and be an acting deacon in one ward and an acting priest in another.[6]

An example of the situation of being "an elder before a deacon" can be seen in the life of Moses Thatcher. Moses was taught the gospel and baptized on December 29, 1856, in Rio Puta, California. On March 23, 1857, he was ordained to the priesthood for the first time, being called to an office of an elder at the age of fifteen.[7]

In 1877, when the shift was in place for young men to receive the Aaronic Priesthood, it was not unusual for the deacons to ready the meetinghouse, which also meant keeping it clean, and included lighting a fire in the stove to warm the building. These young deacons were also expected to chop firewood for the widows and the poor. Deacons, along with the bishop, were also responsible for harvesting the crops of those elders and Seventies serving missions.[8]

In 1907, Hugh B. Brown related his weekly schedule. Part of that schedule was MIA preparation class and choir practice. The one meeting we wouldn't expect to see is Monday evening priesthood meeting.[9]

The year 1910 saw another huge change, the type of change we are currently accustomed to. Priesthood meetings were moved from Monday evenings to Sunday mornings.[10]

NOTES

1. William G. Hartley, "From Men to Boys: LDS Aaronic Priesthood Offices 1829–1996." *Journal of Mormon History* 22 (Spring 1996), 80–136; Lee A. Palmer, *Aaronic Priesthood through the Centuries* (Salt Lake City: Deseret Book, 1964).
2. *History of the Church*, edited by B. H. Roberts (Salt Lake City: Deseret Book, 1902), 7:399.
3. Arnold K. Garr, Donald Q. Cannon, and Richard O. Cowan, *Encyclopedia of Latter-day Saint History* (Salt Lake City: Deseret Book Company, 2000), 1–2.
4. newsroom.churchofjesuschrist.org/article/age-changes-youth-progression-ordination-announced
5. Ronald W. Walker and Doris R. Dant ed., *Nearly Everything Imaginable (*Provo, Utah: BYU Press, 1999), 258.
6. Ibid., 261.
7. Andrew Jenson, *LDS Biographical Encyclopedia* (Salt Lake City: Publishers Press, 1901), 128–29.
8. Ibid., 3:744–745
9. Martha Sonntag Bradley and Mary Brown Firmage Woodward, *4 Zinas* (Signature Books: Salt Lake City, 2000), 392.
10. Leonard J. Arrington and David Bitton, *Saints Without Halos* (Salt Lake City: Signature Books, 1982), 113.).

Primary

I have to be honest. I wasn't a big fan of Primary. We met on Wednesdays after school let out for an hour or so. I can recall dreading Wednesdays. The moment school let out, I dawdled and found any distraction to slow me down on my way home. Without fail my mom would hop in the car and start driving the neighborhood in her attempt to track me down. She had the nose of a bloodhound and found me every single time. I don't know why I did this; it just made matters worse. I had to attend Primary anyway, and coupled with this I received a tongue lashing. It wasn't until years later when I discovered the effects of reverse psychology. I realized I blew it bad. Instead, every Wednesday morning as I was saying good bye to my mom on the way to school, I should have told her to make sure she waited for me because I didn't want to miss Primary. I knew my mom well enough that she would have taken off just to teach me a lesson.

Also, years later, I was glad to see I wasn't the only little boy who didn't particularly care for Primary. I remember leaving church about fifteen years ago when tearing by me in the hallway was a little five-year-old boy. He tore off his tie, crashed through the doors, and jumped off the outside steps to the level of the parking lot, all the while swinging his tie over his head and shouting, "It's over!"

I do recall the anticipation I felt as my graduation from Primary was nearing. One of the requirements to graduate was we had to memorize the Articles of Faith. After being called as a member of the Quorum of the Twelve, Elder L. Tom Perry shared the following now extinct Primary graduation requirement in his general conference talk in April 1974:

> I was reared in a home in which the children were taught great love and respect for the General Authorities of the Church. I remember as I was learning the names of the members of the Council of the Twelve as a Primary graduation requirement, my father spent time and patience to teach me about the lives of each, as well as the required memory work. To this day, I think you can ask me at any tie mot recite the names of those great men . . . and I can repeat them rapidly and remember events in their lives.[1]

Another practice that is long forgotten is the Primary Association's work for the dead. As early as 1922 and into 1923, Primary children ages eight to twelve years performed nearly 50,000 baptisms for the dead in the temples.[2]

NOTES

1. Lawrence R. Flake, *Prophets and Apostles of the Last Dispensation* (Provo, Utah: Religious Study Center, Brigham Young University, 2001), xi.
2. James B. Allen, Jessie L. Embry, Kahlile B. Mehr, *Hearts Turned to the Fathers* (Provo, Utah: BYU Studies, 1995), 119.

Public Works

The departments in the Church today are numerous and varied. However, one would be hard pressed to find the Church Department of Public Works. What better way to employ the influx of immigrants during that first winter in 1847? It's because of the Public Works Department that railroads, meetinghouses, the temple, the Salt Lake Theater, roads, walls, the Tabernacle, canals, telegraph lines, and maybe even ward fences were built. This department continued to 1870, hiring as many as 2,000 men in its heyday.[1]

NOTE

1. Leonard J. Arrington, "Religion and Economics in Mormon History," *BYU Studies,* Vol. 3 No. 3, 1961, 22–23.

Reformation

Brigham Young and other leaders of the Church sensed a waning in religious conviction as indicated in meeting attendance and other commitments such as the payment of tithes and offerings. Based on this observation, in the early fall of 1856, President Young dispatched his counselor, Jedediah M. Grant, to surrounding communities to preach from the pulpit a recommitment to gospel principles. This became termed "the reformation" and started in the northern settlements of Utah, wending its way south to Salt Lake City. As a sign of commitment to the commandments and the expectations of Church members, the Saints were baptized en masse. This re-baptism was an outward sign of an individual's commitment to the gospel. There were those who chose to forgo the ordinance of baptism. A few of these individuals were cut from the Church, with the most cases noted in Britain. It was the reformation that added fuel to the writings of some of those that were antagonistic to the Church.[1] Hannah Tapfield King stated the following about this time period of the Church:

> How well I remember them coming to our house. There was no one at home but Tom Owen and me. They asked if I desired to be questioned in a separate room. I said no, and smiling at Tom I asked him if he did. Poor boy, he was but 16, he looked as guileless as a child and said no. They then proceeded with me. It began, Have you committed murder, ditto, ditto—adultery? Ditto-ditto—robbed?—Spoken slander of your neighbor?—Broken down your neighbor's fences?—Brought your children up in principles of righteousness, etc. [The Catechism] was over a foot in length!! Blessed were those who could answer in innocence.[2]

Sister King shares the following about this practice coming to an end: "At last one Sunday Brigham rose up on the stand peaceful and benign. Told the people to stop their confessions." She would not outright state that the whole episode was misguided. "Only I know it was a fearful ordeal, and fear is a slavish passion and is not begotten by the spirit of God!"[3]

The "reformation" generally ended in 1857, but there was still some preaching and re-baptizing as late as 1858.

Today we can expect General Authorities of the Church armed with speeches centered on reform in our lives. What you won't expect are the General Authorities requesting us to be re-baptized as a an outward sign of our commitment to gospel principles. What we do have, in a sense, is general conference and Church magazines where our leaders encourage us to live Christ-centered lives. The Prophet Joseph Smith once stated that he taught his people righteous principles, and then let them govern themselves.[4]

NOTES

1. Rebecca Bartholomew, *Audacious Women-Early British Mormon Immigrants* (Signature Books: Salt Lake City, 1995), 207–208.
2. Ibid.
3. Ibid.
4. *Messages of the First Presidency,* comp. James R. Clark, 6 vols. (Salt Lake City: Bookcraft, 1965–75), 3:54.

Relief Society

Up to this point in the book you have discovered that the esteemed organization we refer to as the Relief Society, with its illustrious past, has participated along with the priesthood in the establishment of the Church beginning in Nauvoo and carrying on through to Utah and the remainder of the world. This organization was disbanded from 1844 to 1867. Nonetheless, the sisters continued their great work of compassion and charity. It's been seen that the Relief Society from the time of Nauvoo through to the Salt Lake Valley has provided blessings in the form of administrations; served as doctors, nurses, and midwives; prepared the dead for burial; and not only looked after their own in the Church, but also their neighbors, which included their native friends.[1] Nevertheless, it didn't stop there. As you read this section, you will realize, that like the priesthood, the Relief Society organization has also undergone change through the years.

Today we meet in beautiful meetinghouses provided to us by the Church. All the Church asks is that we respect and keep these buildings clean. All organizations and auxiliaries meet under the same roof with up to three, and in some cases, four wards per building. My wife and I were in total amazement when we first moved to Utah and discovered not only the size of the ward geographically but also the fact that in any given city, you can generally drive to two, and in some cases three, different buildings in five minutes from a central point. What really blew us away was when we saw two different chapels sharing the same parking lot. Where my wife and I grew up in Canada, it was nothing like this. In fact, wards in Canada are larger than the combined area of a stake or two in Utah. During the days of Utah Territory, it was not uncommon to see the Relief Society construct its own meeting houses separate from the local chapel. The same took place in Nauvoo, when the Seventies had their own hall/meeting house separate from the regular Sunday worship meetings, generally held in the grove in the open air.[2]

Jane S. Richards, in a talk given at the General Relief Society Conference in 1900, recounted hearing Joseph Smith state that the day would come when the women of the Church would have their own building. To help this materialize, land was donated to this cause by a Brother D. H. Perry of Ogden, Utah, and a nickel fund created in which once a month a nickel was donated by the sisters toward the building for the Relief Society sisters to congregate.[3]

Like today, when the Relief Society sisters no longer meet in their own buildings, so too, the callings one can expect to receive in the Relief Society have evolved. The foundation of the Relief Society has never changed, that of looking out for and taking care of the oppressed and needy. However, due to the times and technologies, there was an overhaul in the positions one could expect to be given as members of this esteemed organization. During the pioneer Church, continuing through to the Utah Territory era and into the early 1900s, it was not uncommon for a member of the Relief Society to be called and set apart to prepare those who died for burial.[4] In fact, in 1921 the Relief Society was charged with the responsibility of creating and organizing the Temple and Burial Clothing Department.[5] As with all things the Relief Society sisters were called on to lead, they definitely didn't disappoint in this endeavor. The finest cloth was saved for both temple and burial clothing; they certainly didn't scrimp.[6]

Another call that a member of the Relief Society could expect over a century or more ago was the position of deaconess. No, this was not a priesthood position. However, it was fashioned much after the deacons in the Aaronic Priesthood. This calling entailed the preparation of the meetinghouse for Relief Society meetings as far as organization and cleanliness were concerned.[7] Other callings in the organization included: "Presidentess; two counselors; a secretary and a treasurer; a council of teachers with a presidentess and a secretary; whose responsibility it was to visit the sisters in the ward, caring for the needy and collecting donations; a deaconess to prepare the meeting place; messengers to run errands; superintendents of work to provide for the handwork; a board of apprizers to assess donations; and a commission mechantess to sell or exchange what the society received or made."[8]

As different as it may seem, the Relief Society, at least during the Nauvoo years of the Church, worked alongside men building homes. In a sense, they still do this today. I remember back in the early 1970s when Olds, Alberta, was constructing a chapel. My dad was a contractor by trade and was asked by the stake presidency if he would supervise the building of this chapel. Every Saturday my dad would load up his tools and me and make the fifty-mile drive north of Calgary, and by use of the volunteer force that showed up that day, construct their new building. Because I was too young to swing the hammer, my dad gave me the job of keeping the construction site clean and straightening bent nails. As good as this was, the most anticipated part of the day was the lunch provided by the local Relief Society sisters. I also recall home teaching a number of years ago an elderly widow in our ward. Shortly after World War II ended, she and her engineer husband were sent by the government to northwestern Montana during the construction of the Hungry Horse Dam (just south of Glacier National Park). She was telling me that at this time the Columbia Falls Branch in the area was saving for a new chapel, one that wasn't rented, but could call their own. She said the Relief Society committed to not using electricity in the evenings, but rather candles, and using the money saved toward the construction of their new chapel. She also said the Relief Society sisters washed their clothing with wash boards rather than using their electric washers as another way to accumulate money toward the building of the chapel.

Other projects that the Relief Society was called on during the earlier years of the Church included economic ventures such as the "establishment of cooperative stores, developing silk manufacturing industries, and arranging for storage of many thousands of bushels of wheat."[9]

Another major function of the Relief Society during the 1800s and into the 1900s was the medical well-being of not just its members but the general Church membership. The Relief Society was mandated with the training of midwives. Classes were offered for the sisters to learn this skill. Some voluntarily took it upon themselves to acquire this knowledge, whereas in others cases women were called and set apart by bishops, developing this skill to benefit the mothers of their respective wards. It didn't stop at midwifery, but extended much further than this. In 1899, Dr. Margaret "Maggie" Curtis Shipp Roberts taught the first class in nursing. Forty-eight students graduated from the Relief Society Nursing School that first year, infusing Utah with many more people trained to monitor the health of the Saints. This class continued far into the 1900s.[10] In addition to the local educating of mid-wives and nurses, the Relief Society funded and sponsored others interested in attending eastern colleges to gain the skills necessary to become doctors. Due to this work of the Relief Society, it was said at the turn of the century that

Utah had more trained women doctors than any other culture in any other region in the United States. This was a huge endeavor. The fact that Utah did not have a medical school at the time required detail planning on how those at home could assist with the family of those who chose to separate themselves temporarily while they gained the skills to become doctors. The returns were huge though in the future health care of the Church.[11]

Similar to the General Authorities handling multiple callings, so too, this also existed in the Relief Society. For example, Belle Spafford was called to the general board of the Relief Society in 1935, while at the same time serving in her ward Relief Society and as a counselor in her stake Relief Society presidency.[12]

The following is an example of the outstanding service by ward Relief Societies in general, more specifically the Fifteenth Ward Relief Society in Salt Lake City. Sarah Kimball shares her thoughts:

> November 1868 was no small occasion, at least for Sarah Kimball, who was provided with a silver trowel and mallet and an assembly of Fifteenth Ward men and women with whom to share her vision of woman's work. Her speech was carefully recorded:
>
> "I appear before you in this interesting occasion on behalf of the Female Relief Society to express thanks to the Almighty God that the wheels of progress have been permitted to run until they have brought us to a more extended field of useful labor for female minds and hands.
>
> "With feelings of humility and gratitude I stand upon this consecrated rock, and contemplate the anticipated result of the completion of this unpretending edifice (which I will here call "Our Store"), the upper story of which will be dedicated to art and science; the lower story to commerce or trade. I view this as a stepping stone to similar enterprises on a grander scale."[13]

She then states that the Relief Society had in its possession in meetinghouses and land valued at just shy of $100,000 in the Utah Territory, Idaho, Arizona, Canada, and Mexico. She further lists the Fifteenth Ward's Relief Society's accomplishments, which included the manufacturing of woolen cloth, carpet rags, spools of cotton, baby stockings, crewel and braid, dried fruits, valentines, buttons, shoes, and moccasins, all of which were sold and used to pay for their new building. She goes on to say that the sisters of her ward were instrumental in the purchase of the ward organ, a granary, contributions to the Perpetual Emigration fund, donations to both the Salt Lake and Logan Temples and Deseret Hospital, sending assistance to victims in the Chicago fire, sending the *Woman's Exponent* to poor British sisters, establishing a ward kindergarten, paying the tuition of poor children, and founding a ward library.[14]

Louisa B. Pratt wrote:

> Great good was done in reliving the wants of the poor, in visitation of the sick, in fasting and prayer for the unfortunate. When one of the members was sick it was, and still is our custom, to fast and pray for their recovery. To wash and anoint them, lay our hands upon them and rebuke the disease. This to the unbeliever in the restoration of the Priesthood might seem a daring thing for woman to assume a right to perform. But when the Savior said, "These signs shall follow them that believe, in my name shall they cast our devils, etc." he made no distinction of sexes.[15]

When the Relief Society was first organized in Nauvoo in March of 1842, the name the sisters chose to call their organization was the Female Relief Society. Today, membership is automatic based on age, but this hasn't always been the case. When the Relief Society was first formed, invitation into the society was by the vote of its membership.[16]

NOTES

1. churchofjesuschrist.org/study/manual/gospel-topics-essays/joseph-smiths-teachings-about-priesthood-temple-women?lang=eng
2. Kenneth W. Godfrey, Audrey M. Godfrey, and Jill Mulvay Derr, *Women's Voices: An Untold History of The Latter-day Saints 1830–1900* (Salt Lake City: Deseret Book Company, 1982), 288.
3. Vicky Burgess-Olsen, *Sister Saints* (Vicky Burgess-Olsen: 1978), 191–92.
4. Mary Wheeler Chadwick, Biographical Sketch, 6, ed. Thersa C. Lowder, in Jeanette S. Greenwell, comp., *Abraham and Mary Wheeler Chadwick* (N.P., n.d.), 367.
5. Jill Mulvay Derr, Janath Russell Cannon, and Maureen Ursenbach Beecher, *Women of Covenant: The Story of Relief Society* (Salt Lake City: Deseret Book, 1992), 198.
6. Seymour B. Young, Diary, July 27, 1921, typescript, Church History Library.
7. Ronald W. Walker and Doris R. Dant ed., *Nearly Everything Imaginable* (Provo, Utah: BYU Press, 1999), 263.
8. Vicky Burgess-Olsen, *Sister Saints* (Vicky Burgess-Olsen: 1978), 30.
9. Ibid.

10. *Chronicles of Courage,* comp. by Lesson Committee (Salt Lake City: Daughters of Utah Pioneers, 1992), 3:134.
11. Lesson Committee, Museum Memories—Daughters of Utah Pioneers (Salt Lake City, Talon Printing, 2010), 2:3.
12. Ibid..
13. Reid L. Neilson and Ronald W. Walker, *Reflections of A Mormon Historian-Leonard J. Arrington on the New Mormon History (*Norman, Oklahoma: The Arthur H. Clark Company, 2006), 213.
14. Susan Easton Black and Mary Jane Woodger, *Women of Character* (American Fork, Utah: Covenant Communications, Inc., 2011), 312.
15. Vicky Burgess-Olsen, *Sister Saints* (Vicky Burgess-Olsen: 1978), 30–32.
16. Ibid., 50.

For additional information see, Jill Mulvay Derr, et al. Women of the Covenant: The Story of Relief Society (Salt Lake City: Deseret Book, 1992).

Sacrament

On one occasion I journeyed the sixteen hours north to visit my dad and dying mother, who could no longer attend sacrament meeting in their small branch. Those assigned to minister to her and my dad brought and administered the sacrament each Sunday. I happened to be there on one occasion when the bread was blessed and passed. The slice of bread was torn in half. My mom broke a piece of bread off one of the halves and partook. Later, after the sacrament was complete, one of their ministering brothers explained that this is the way the sacrament was administered at the time of the Savior. I had read this but had never up until this time seen the sacrament passed this way. According to Zebedee Coltrin, an early member of the Church, it appears this is the same way the sacrament was administered in the School of the Prophets:

> The salutation as written in the Doctrine and Covenants [D&C 88:136–141] was carried out at that time, and at every meeting, and the

> washing of feet was attended to, the sacrament was also administered at times when Joseph appointed, after the ancient order; that is, warm bread to break easy was provided and broken into pieces as large as my fist and each person had a glass of wine and sat and ate the bread and drank the wine; and Joseph said that was the way that Jesus and his disciples partook of the bread and wine. And this was the order of the church anciently and until the church went into darkness. Every time we were called together to attend to any business, we came together in the morning about sunrise, fasting and partook of the sacrament each time, and before going to school we washed ourselves and put on clean linen.[1]

At the end of Brigham Young's presidency, some changes were instituted regarding the sacrament. In a letter from the First Presidency dated July 11, 1877, bishops were encouraged to begin passing the sacrament to children in Sunday School so that they "become accustomed to the importance of this ordinance."[2] So why weren't children included in the participation of the sacrament prior to this date? According to the *Juvenile Instructor,* much had to do with the size of the meetinghouses. There simply wasn't room to have all sit during the Sunday meetings, so consequently, the children were generally left at home. With the organization of the Sunday School, this soon changed.[3]

During these years it was common during the passing of the sacrament for either a talk given at the pulpit or singing by the congregation, which may be in a kneeling, sitting, or standing position. It wasn't until May 2, 1946, that the First Presidency issued the following statement: "The ideal condition is to have absolute quiet during the passing of the sacrament, and that we look with disfavor upon vocal solos, duets, group signing, or instrumental music during the administration of this sacred ordinance."[4]

When the Saints first entered the valley, it was common to partake of the sacrament on a monthly basis. It wasn't until the 1850s that the sacrament was administered weekly.[5]

There were also times when the sacrament was withheld. Such occasions was during the Reformation (1856–57) and immediately following this, during the Utah War (1857–58).[6] The rationale for the Reformation was obvious. It was a time to have the Saints reflect and conform to the teachings of the Savior, to set in place a Christ-centered life. After the outward sign of re-baptism, the ordinance was again administered. But what about the Utah War? Why would federal troops in the Salt Lake Valley cause a stop of the passing of the sacrament? If there were no meetings, then the sacrament wasn't going to be passed.[7] Brigham Young terminated meetings for a time because of fear that over the pulpit some Saints might speak out against the troops and government, adding to the friction on a situation that was already teetering on a powder keg. Brigham Young encouraged prayer meetings with the added caution to "be careful to control all that may be said." Bishop Hunter, the presiding bishop of the Church, felt the same uneasiness when he stated, "For an enthusiastic Mormon is more dangerous than an Apostate." In early August of 1859 Brigham Young lifted the ban and encouraged meetings to be held throughout the territory.[8]

Throughout the Utah Territory years the method of passing the sacrament was much different than what we are accustomed to today. Currently, we would expect twelve- and thirteen-year-old young men to pass the sacrament to the congregation. In most wards, there are enough Aaronic Priesthood-aged youth to accomplish this. However, the last two wards I have lived in, the Melchizedek Priesthood also lends a hand due to the lack in numbers of Aaronic-aged youth. I can see going forward, due to the demographics of the Church (people having smaller families), that the Melchizedek Priesthood holders will be called on more to assist. The following is from a bishop in an 1874 meeting:

"At 2 PM I administered the sacrament in the New Tabernacle assisted by my 2 council[ors] and [Acting] Teachers." Some wards blessed bread and wine first, then passed both at the same time. In other wards, bishops decided "to bless the bread and wine at the Sacrament according to the universal custom" instead of "blessing both before distributing either."[9]

It was during an 1854 meeting when the bread was blessed. As the bread was passed to the congregation, Brigham Young stood at the pulpit and preached a sermon, stopping in mid-sermon so that he could bless the wine. While the wine was passed, Brigham continued the sermon.[10]

NOTES

1. Minutes, Salt Lake City School of the Prophets, October 3, 1883.
2. lds.org/ensign/1988/04/remembering-the-saviors-atonement?lang=eng
3. Ronald W. Walker and Doris R. Dant, ed. *Nearly Everything Imaginable* (Provo, Utah: BYU Press, 1999), 253.
4. lds.org/ensign/1988/04/remembering-the-saviors-atonement?lang=eng
5. Bishops Minutes, February 25, 1852, comments concerning Salt Lake's Thirteenth Ward in Ronald W. Walker and Doris R. Dant ed., 268.
6. Brigham Young to George A. Smith, January 26, 1852 in *Journal History*, January 26, 1857 in Ronald W. Walker and Doris R. Dant ed, 268.
7. Ronald W. Walker and Doris R. Dant ed., 268.
8. Ibid.
9. Ibid., 269.
10. Ibid.

School of the Prophets

In what is now Doctrine and Covenants 88, the Lord instructed the elders of the Church that before proceeding to "go forth among the Gentiles for the last time," they were to "tarry" and learn. This led to the establishment of "a school for the Prophets."[1] Interestingly, the phrase "School of the Prophets" is not unique to this Church. In fact, during the seventeenth and eighteenth century, Yale and Harvard Universities trained clergy in seminaries that "were referred to at times as schools of the prophets." This continued into the nineteenth century during the religious revival movement identified as the "Second Great Awakening."[2]

The School of the Prophets that Joseph Smith organized in Kirtland, Ohio, was considered the first school for adult education in America.[3] Like the Relief Society, the school was disbanded when the Saints were pushed from Nauvoo. Also, like the Relief Society, it was reorganized by Brigham Young in Salt Lake City in 1867. The Salt Lake and Kirtland schools followed a similar curriculum with instruction in both theology and secular courses. In a sense, the School of the Prophets expanded its influence in Salt Lake City through involvement in a number of ventures, such as raising funds for the Perpetual Emigration Fund, promoting the construction of the railroad from Salt Lake City to Ogden, and other endeavors that benefitted the Saints in Utah.[4] As named, the School of the Prophets fails to exist today. Because of this we can state that this is a change, but not really. The Church has always had a firm conviction in educating its people, whether that be in the gospel or secular knowledge. The Church has maintained its academies, colleges, universities, seminaries, and institutes.

NOTES

1. Joseph Smith "Letter to William W. Phelps, 11 January 1833, josephsmithpapers.org, seechurchofjesuschrist.org/study/manual/revelations-in-context/a-school-and-an-endowment?lang=eng
2. Joseph Darowski, "School of the Prophets: An Early American Tradition," *Mormon Historical Studies,* vol. 9 no. 1 (Spring 2008), 1–13. See churchofjesuschrist.org/study/manual/revelations-in-context/a-school-and-an-endowment?lang=eng
3. Leonard J. Arrington, *Great Basin Kingdom: An Economic History of the Latter-day Saints,* 1830–1900 (Cambridge: Harvard University Press), 245–251.
4. Leonard J. Arrington, *Great Basin Kingdom: An Economic History of the Latter-day Saints,* 1830–1900, 245–251.

Sealings for the Living

As you read this next story from the autobiography of Mosiah Hancock, understand that he was born April 9, 1834:

> After the death of the Prophet, the mob spent their fury on the Twelve and a few others. The Brethren pushed the work on the Temple; and the Gospel was preached; and every Saint was busy doing all he could to help the work along. Although I was very young, I was on guard many a night, and gladly did I hail with

> many of the Saints, the completion of the temple. On about January 10, 1846, I was privileged to go in the temple and receive my washings and anointings. I was sealed to a lovely young girl named Mary [Dunn], who was about my age, but it was with the understanding that we were not to live together as man and wife until we were 16 years of age. The reason that some were sealed so young was because we knew that we would have to go West and wait many a long time for another temple.
>
> We left the Indian Mills on May 14, 1848, and we left Winter Quarters on May 18th. While we were camped at Winter Quarters, Mary Dunn came to our camp and wanted to go with us, but mother said we could not take her because we had no room. Mary's mother had died and her father had gotten a stepmother for his children. She came with her bundle of clothes to our wagon, and with what joy I hailed my noble, beautiful wife! But Mary had to go, and oh what sorrow as I saw her depart. We were separated for life.[1]

It's difficult for us today to wrap our minds around two twelve-year-olds married in the temple for time and eternity. However, if living under the same circumstances, the marriage of Mosiah to Mary made sense. First, people were married far younger than what we are accustomed to, and there was the stipulation that they were not to live together as husband and wife until they were sixteen. The larger factor was the fact the Saints were being pushed into the wilderness not knowing when the next temple would be erected. Because of this, other provisions were made under desperate circumstances. For instance, without a temple, temple sealings were performed in Winter Quarters in Willard Richards' octagon house for members of the Mormon Battalion who, not knowing what the future held, separated themselves from family and pushed through on their trek. This also applied to the terminally ill.[2]

NOTES

1. boap.org/LDS/Early-Saints/MHancock.html
2. *History of the Saints,* Harley, William G., ed. (American Fork, Utah: Covenant Communications, 2012), 63.

Stakes

Today we're accustomed to approximately eight to ten wards per stake. This hasn't always been the case through modern history in The Church of Jesus Christ of Latter-day Saints. For example, by 1900, the Salt Lake Stake had fifty-one wards and approximately 11,000 Saints when the Jordan and Granite Stakes were organized.[1]

Another oddity is that prior to 1877, the Salt Lake City Stake, with Angus M. Cannon as stake president, held superiority over the only other stake (Weber Stake) to the point that the Salt Lake Stake approved other individuals called in the Weber Stake. With the realignment of the priesthood in 1877, this all changed and all stakes were given equal authority.[2]

NOTES

1. *Church History In The Fulness Of Time* (Salt Lake City: Published by The Church of Jesus Christ of Latter-day Saints, 1993), 459; *"Manuscript History of Salt Lake Stake"* LDS Church Historical Department, Salt Lake City; *The Story of the Salt Lake Stake, The Church of Jesus Christ of Latter-day Saints: 150 Years of History, 1847–1997* (Salt Lake City: Salt Lake Stake, 1997).
2. Donald Q. Cannon and David J. Whittaker, *Supporting Saints: Life Stories of Nineteenth-Century Mormons* (Salt Lake City: Bookcraft Inc., 1985), 384.

Sunday School

A Sunday School was organized in Logan, Utah, in 1866, but it was not a ward activity; it was a city-wide institution, unaffiliated with any one ward. Also, unfamiliar to us, when the Sunday Schools were first organized, it was not uncommon for academic subjects to be taught. Part of the issue was the lack of teaching material specifically designed to educate on religious topics.[1] I'm sure it's difficult to fathom secular subjects taught during Sunday School, but to add to this uniqueness was examination day of the material covered.[2]

Common for ward Sunday Schools in early-day-Utah was the production of a Sunday School newspapers. Louisa G. Richards, in the fall of 1869, edited the *Smithfield Sunday School Gazette.* Themes that she centered the paper on were "Attend Sabbath School and pay attention" and "Attend Sunday School and preserve order."[3]

NOTES

1. *New Views on Mormon History*, Edited by Davis Bitton and Maureen Usenbach Beecher (Salt Lake City, University of Utah Press, 1987), 150.
2. Arnold K. Garr, Donald Q. Cannon, and Richard O. Cowan, *Encyclopedia of Latter-day Saint History* (Salt Lake City: Deseret Book Company, 2000), 73.
3. Vicky Burgess-Olsen, *Sister Saints* (Vicky Burgess-Olsen: 1978), 439–440.

Sustaining Votes

Today we are accustomed to raising our hand in sustaining votes to previous decisions determined in meetings by Church leaders as they discussed Church business behind closed council doors. This current practice saves valuable time for ward and stake meetings and centers the attention of the meeting on the worship of Christ. However, this wasn't always the case. Prior to a conference of the Church held on April 6, 1839, in England, business was transacted first during the meeting by those in attendance. In many cases, if you read of the marathon-style meetings the early Saints were accustomed to, this could be part of the reason. I imagine some decisions were easy and consumed little time. Nevertheless, on the flip side of the coin, some decisions took hours to come to a resolution.[1]

NOTES

1. James B. Allen, et. al., *Men with a Mission* (Salt Lake City: Deseret Book, 1992), 301.

Tabernacle—Salt Lake City

The first time I saw the Tabernacle on Temple Square was in 1974. This was the end destination after our family traveled three days east from Calgary to Ontario to visit my mom's side of the family. The concluding portion of the vacation was Church history related when we followed the Saints west from Palmyra, to Kirtland, to Nauvoo, to Missouri, to Winter Quarters, and on through along the Mormon Trail (maybe not the same order as the Saints did it, but regardless we visited the historic sites). I remember standing in the Tabernacle for the first time in my young life, enthralled by the size of the building. Little did I realize what was to happen in the not too distant future across the street from Temple Square. I wish I was older at the time, only because I failed to understand the significance of the building I was standing in. I was amazed more by the size, rather than the religious importance the building held and the sacrifice rendered by the Saints to construct this, which coincided at the same time the Salt Lake Temple was under construction. I was astounded when a pin was dropped and it could be heard. A few years later, in 1977 I sat in the Tabernacle with approximately three hundred other new missionaries enjoying *Music and the Spoken Word*. I was thrilled to see the Choir at Temple Square for the first time live along with the fabled organ. I'm sure early Utah Territory Saint Evan Stephens felt the same thrill.

Evan Stephens, born June 29, 1854, on occasion went to Salt Lake City to hear the organ in the Tabernacle. He stayed at the campground in the tithing yard (the location of the current Joseph Smith Memorial Building), crossed the street to Temple Square, and enjoy whatever concert he came to see. The following is from Evan: "It was during this visit that I entered the Tabernacle in true country style, minus coat. When under the shadow of the great organ, I was asked to return to my hotel and don that article which was, even then in Salt Lake City, deemed essential on such an occasion."[1]

NOTES

1. Daughters of Utah Pioneers, *Chronicles of Courage* (Salt Lake City: Lesson Committee, 1993), V4:299–300.

Tabernacle—St. George

Welcoming ministers from other religions to preach from the Church of Jesus Christ of Latter-day Saints pulpits is not new. This is a privilege that Joseph Smith extended to other faiths. Joseph Smith taught religious tolerance, which Brigham Young continued, allowing those of other persuasions to preach to the Saints. What might not be so well known is the Catholic Mass held in the St. George Tabernacle.

In 1879, the Catholic Church was invited to use the St. George Tabernacle to celebrate Mass. Why the tabernacle? It was because, as Father Scanlon (a Catholic priest) stated, he did not have a building or a choir to celebrate it. Erastus Snow granted Father Scanlon the use of the tabernacle and offered his house to provide accommodations for Catholic officials attending from Salt Lake City. To solve the choir issue, the local Saints provided the choir and spent numerous hours learning to sing the Latin Mass.[1]

NOTES

1. Lesson Committee, *Museum Memories* (Salt Lake City: Talon Printing, 2009), 373–74.

Temples

After the conclusion of temple dedications, its doors are closed to temple recommend holders only. This is the way it is today, but it hasn't always been the case. In April 1934, a representative from the king of England was given a tour of the Alberta Temple, even though it was a dedicated temple.[1]

The temple is the house of the Lord. When inside, reverence is the rule, with low whispers if communication is necessary. It may seem odd for a brass band to perform in the temple and for couples in attendance to dance. The following is a journal account of this occasion:

> On February 9, 1846, the band gave its final performance in Nauvoo. At the request of Brigham Young, they met in the upper room of the temple and played a few tunes for the assembled people. Young arose and informed the members that he thought it would do no harm to have a little recreational singing, as long as it was done in righteousness. He then called on the Lord to take charge of the meeting, and the men and women danced.[2]

Ida Cook tells of adult education classes held in the Logan Temple in 1885. These were monthly, one-hour classes with instructions in theology, government, history, languages, economics, and philosophy.[3]

Today the temples are dedicated at the completion of construction. This was true of the Nauvoo temple in addition to five other dedications during various stages of constructions. The following is a listing of the six dedications the Nauvoo Temple received:

1. November, 8, 1841—The temporary baptismal font is dedicated in the basement of the temple by the Prophet Joseph Smith.
2. October 5, 1845—Brigham Young dedicates all work completed to that date including the exterior of the temple.
3. November 30, 1845—The attic is dedicated by Brigham Young.
4. January 7, 1846—Brigham Young again dedicates all the work completed to this date in addition to dedicating an alter for the purposes of sealings in the attic of the temple.
5. April 30, 1846—During a private ceremony, Joseph Young dedicates the temple.

6. May 1, 1846—The Nauvoo Temple is dedicated during a public dedication by Orson Hyde.[4]

During the Kirtland years of the Church, the term "temple" was not used. Rather, the Saints referred to the Kirtland Temple merely as the "Lord's House." The word "chapel" was also infrequently used.[5]

It's fascinating that temple workers in the newly dedicated St. George Temple received a monthly income for serving. In a sense, this was looked as an old-age compensation for those who had given so much voluntary service to the Church in their younger years.[6]

The following is from the life of Chauncey West. It's intriguing that he was ordained an elder in the temple. Also notice the length of the endowment sessions. This occurred in 1895:

> The sixth of April was a special day, a day of beginnings. After a tour of the city and county building, "I met Grandpa on my way home (to where I were staying), and it was my wish that I be ordained an Elder Of The Church Of Jesus Christ Of Latter-day Saints, this day, it being the sixty-fifth anniversary of the organization of the Church.
>
> I got [stake] president R. Clawson's consent, and went to the Temple and was ordained in the Temple an Elder by Grandpa (the President of the Salt Lake Temple) and LeRoi Snow. 7:30 o'clock.
>
> We then went to the concert in the Tabernacle, given by the choir (Salt Lake City Tabernacle choir numbering about one thousand). The large choir singing, and the immense organ screeching, fairly shook the Tabernacle.
>
> I enjoyed the concert, and was well entertained. After it was over we went out, and the Large World's fair search lights now in the city was turned on us. It was so strong that I would turn my back to it. We watched them (two) for some time, and had them turned on us going home.
>
> Chauncey attended all sessions of general conference, visited the theater, the Deseret Museum, the science building at the University of Utah, and attended a class in "Doctrinal Theology" at the LDS College. Then he and Le Roi had lunch in the temple and were given an extraordinary tour.
>
> We . . . went in the six towers as far as we could safely get. We almost went to the top of the west middle tower, up past the last strait projection. I never care to be in a nicer place than the Temple. When we came back down I sat in the chair made for the President of The Temple (my Grandpa). It was as soft and easy as life could wish to rest upon. I walked over the top of the Temple. We came out after three hours walking and seeing. I went through as thoroughly as anybody and more than visitors and workers.

He returned the temple the following day and was baptized on behalf of fourteen deceased persons. "I then went around in the Temple for a while, and enjoyed myself very much under its holy roof."

On April 10 Chauncey arrived at the temple at 8:50 A.M. and attended a preliminary meeting in the annex. "It was fine. I then prepared myself to go through the Temple. It was the crowdest day that there had ever been in the Temple, I getting through the first one, at about 4:30.

The next morning Chauncey "went through [the temple] for a dead person," in a shorter, six-and-a-half hour session."[7]

NOTES

1. Richard Neitzel Holzapfel, et al., *On This Day In The Church* (Salt Lake City: Eagle Gate, 2000), 83.
2. Lesson Committee, *Museum Memories* (Salt Lake City: Talon Printing, 2009), 199.
3. Vicky Burgess-Olsen, *Sister Saints* (Vicky Burgess-Olsen: 1978), 254.
4. Don F. Colvin, *Nauvoo Temple: A Story of Faith* (American Fork, Utah; Covenant Communications, 2002), 245–51.
5. ldschurchtemples.com/kirtland/; Ronald K. Esplin and Sharon E. Nielsen, The Record of the Twelve, 1835, *BYU Studies*, Vol. 51, No. 1, 2012, 6.
6. M. Guy Bishop, "A Great Little Saint: A Brief Look at the Life of Henry William Bigler," *BYU Studies*, 30:4, 36.
7. Leonard J. Arrington and David Bitton, *Saints Without Halos* (Salt Lake City: Signature Books, 1982), 102–103.

Tithing

Today, tithing donations in the Church are cut and dry, black and white. However, they tended to be more complex during the early years of The Church of Jesus Christ of Latter-day Saints. During the 1830s in the Church, members "understood tithing to refer to any amount of freely consecrated goods or money."[1] In September 1837 the Kirtland bishopric, using the Malachi 3:10 promise in the Old Testament, taught "the Saints to bring their tithes into the store house."[2] Shortly after this the bishopric in Missouri asked that "each household should offer a tithe of

2 percent of its annual worth after paying the household's debts."[3] It was also at this time that the Church considered the raising of another temple, in the state of Missouri. While contemplating this endeavor, Joseph Smith called for a meeting in July of 1838. It was during this meeting when Joseph Smith received revelations that are currently canonized as section 119 in the Doctrine and Covenants, the Lord's call for the tithing of this people, and section 120, the disposition of tithes.[4]

Since this time, and continuing into the Utah Territorial years, interesting situations have occurred. When we read about them, we realize that even though tithing still exists in the Church, the manner in which it was practiced has changed with time.

Savalla Bishop Melville, daughter of William Henry Bishop, wrote the following: "Grandfather followed his trade of smithing, was delegated by the Church to do work for the Indians for tithing."[5] It's difficult to tell, based on the autobiography account, exactly what year or years William would have worked for the natives in lieu of tithing since no date is given. The first date mentioned after the above account is when he takes a trip to New York in 1880. We are left to assume it was somewhere between the time he entered the Salt Lake Valley to the 1880 date.

According to Lauritz Smith, a member of the Draper Ward, his bishop determined each member's contribution for tithing. This may seem strange since the bishop may not have known what each individual in the ward earned as income. To be honest, I'm thinking this may have been more like a ward budget assessment that I was familiar with as a young man. It just might be that it was termed "tithe" rather than donation.[6]

Parley P. Pratt explains the different types of tithes that the Saints were expected to pay (property, increase, and labor) during an October 7, 1849 speech:

> To fulfill the law of tithing a man should make out and lay before the [Presiding] Bishop [then Newell K. Whitney] a schedule of all his property, and pay him the tenth of it. When he has tithed his principal once, he has no occasion to tithe again [on that property]. But the next year he must pay one-tenth of his increase of cattle, money, goods and trade. A member also owed the tenth of his time—a labor tithe of each tenth day of man, young man, and work animals and wagons for the days not devoted to producing income or increase.[7]

The principle behind labor tithing is an interesting aspect of the history of this commandment in the Church. After reading the rules and stipulations, you may feel like me and realize how much less complicated we have it today. This principle was first encouraged during the Nauvoo years of the Church. If a man worked nine days, the tenth day was devoted to the Lord. The outward sign was the individual volunteering labor at the temple construction site. Labor tithing could also be used to pay off regular tithing in kind. A man could also hire another man to fulfill his labor tithing. Labor tithing was not a stipulation on the individual only, but also his tools, equipment, livestock, and wagons. Labor tithes followed the Saints west to the Salt Lake Valley. It was common for projects read from the pulpit, which men could devote their labor tithes to. Some men held their labor tithing back until the winter months. Brigham Young had an issue with this due to the few projects available during the colder months of the year. He encouraged men to give their labor when the projects were available and worked on during the spring, summer, and fall. It's because of labor tithing that temples, tabernacles, roads, canals, public buildings, and fences were built. Other projects that were derived from labor tithing included serving on the down and back teams, meeting immigrants at the rail heads and transporting them to the Salt Lake Valley, taking supplies to the needy natives in the area, delivering the mail, serving as militia men during the Indian Wars, serving during the Utah War, and rescuing stranded immigrants and the local poor.[8]

It's obvious that little tithing was paid using cash. During 1854, the tithing yard took in total receipts worth $143,372 of which only $25,000 was in cash. Much of what was used to pay tithing was perishable, so an efficient system was established not to discard anything given to the tithing office.[9]

During the Utah Territory years, ward clerks did not exist to monitor tithing. It's remarkable that in 1873 Bishop Elijah F. Sheets used his ward teachers (home teachers) to go into the homes of the families in his ward, and determine how much income was earned in the home and how much tithing was paid. Whereas today, the bishop meets with the families in his ward during tithing settlement, it appears this responsibility fell on the shoulders of the home teachers, at least in the Salt Lake Valley Eighth Ward.[10] I had to chuckle to myself when for the first time in my Church career, my bishop announced at the beginning of tithing settlement season a new way he devised to conduct it.

He encouraged the families of the ward to use any type of technology to contact him to discuss their tithing, anything from texting, to instant messaging on Facebook to Skype, including the traditional means of sitting and visiting with him in his office.

NOTES

1. churchofjesuschrist.org/study/manual/revelations-in-context/the-tithing-of-my-people?lang=eng
2. churchofjesuschrist.org/study/manual/revelations-in-context/the-tithing-of-my-people?lang=eng
3. Minute Book 2, Dec. 6–7 1837, 89–90, josephsmithpapers.org
4. churchofjesuschrist.org/study/manual/revelations-in-context/the-tithing-of-my-people?lang=eng
5. Autobiography of Henry William Bishop, Typescript HBLL, boap.org/
6. *Peace Like A River,* The Historical and Spiritual Journey of The Isaac M. Stewart Family, Compiled and Edited By David H. Epperson (Salt Lake City, 2007), 49.
7. *Journal History*, 7 October 1849, Archives, Historical Department, The Church of Jesus Christ of Latter-day Saints, Salt Lake City.
8. Donald Q. Cannon and David J. Whittaker, *Supporting Saints: Life Stories of Nineteenth-Century Mormons* (Salt Lake City: Bookcraft Inc., 1985), 283, 286.
9. Robert Mullen, *The Latter-day Saints: The Mormons Yesterday and Today* (New York: Doubleday, 1966), 133.
10. Donald Q. Cannon and David J. Whittaker, *Supporting Saints: Life Stories of Nineteenth-Century Mormons* (Salt Lake City: Bookcraft Inc., 1985), 260–61.

Titles

Recently our prophet encouraged us to drop the term "Mormon" when referring to ourselves or the church we belong to. The term "Mormon" has been applied to us since the days of Joseph Smith. One might also have heard on occasion, shortly after the Church was organized, the term "Mormonite." We know that the term "Mormon" is a nickname given to us because of our belief in the Book of Mormon. We are accustomed to using many titles in the Church. Brother, Sister, Bishop, and President are some of the more common titles and are acceptable. However, when it comes to the name of the Lord's Church, using the term "Mormon" is never acceptable. During Brigham Young's presidency, other inappropriate titles were applied. On August 7, 1863, Edmund C. Briggs and Alexander McCord entered Salt Lake City as two missionaries for the Reorganized Church of Jesus Christ of Latter-day Saints. They referred to themselves as "Josephites," or the "Reorganization," and spoke of those members belonging to The Church of Jesus Christ of Latter-day Saints as "Brighamites."[1] Some Restoration groups still use the term "Brighamites," today. As mentioned earlier, during a Utah census the titles "Gentile" and "Josephites" were used to distinguish an individual's status.

NOTE

1. Steven L. Shields, The Early Community of Christ Mission to "Redeem" the Church in Utah, *Journal of Mormon History*, Fall 2014, 159–60.

Tramp Department

While in Brigham City, Lorenzo Snow organized a cooperative enterprise with the goal of employing all who wanted to work, paying them as high as possible in goods. This enterprise included numerous types of industry, many of which were typical of early Church settlements. What was unique to the enterprise was something called the "Tramp Department." The purpose was to provide work for passing "hoboes" (wandering men, generally looking for work by traveling town to town).[1]

NOTE

1. James B. Allen et. al., *The Presidents of the Church* (Salt Lake City: Deseret Book Company, 1986), 166.

Wards

The ward as we know it today evolved over time. During the Palmyra and Kirtland years of the Church, wards failed to exist. In the early Church, the entire community (stake) would meet each Sunday, whereas the bishop's wards were districts mandated to the caring of the poor, rather than separate congregations. It wouldn't be until the Nauvoo years when wards took on more of the look that we are accustomed to today. With the influx in population in Utah Territory during the 1850s and 1860s, there was a move away from the entire city/town meeting as a congregation toward more easily manageable numbers and area. During the early Salt Lake Valley years, in some places, the ward was the settlement and the valley that housed the settlement was considered the stake. Never in these years was population of the ward an issue. It wasn't like today when the ward gets so large that it is divided. It was Lorenzo Snow, and continuing through to Joseph F. Smith, that ward sizes were made smaller to give those attending the ward an opportunity to serve. This was not an option with the larger wards, when literally thousands could belong.[1]

George Q. Cannon shares the following recollection:

> After the lots were given out to the people a united effort was made to fence the city. Instead of fencing each lot separately, each ward [an area of nine blocks] was fenced in one field, and each owner of a lot in a ward built his proportion of fence. This made the work of fencing the lots comparatively easy, and it answered every purpose for several seasons. The streets were all kept open, but not at their present width. The owners of lots cultivated the streets in front of their premises, leaving no more than a sufficient space for travel.[2]

In 1849, two years after the Saints entered the valley, Salt Lake City was divided, not into wards but rather into what they referred to as "bishop wards." There were nineteen such wards.[3]

If I asked, could you name your ward police? Probably not, but don't worry, neither can I. Why not? Simply because ward police no longer exist. There's little reason to have a number of brethren walk the ward to ensure it's safety; the municipality we live in has us covered. This from the life of Henry Crow:

Soon after his arrival in Utah he located in the Eleventh Ward, Salt Lake City, which was his home until his death. Soldiers who were located at Fort Douglas frequently were guilty of disturbing the peace and robbing the gardens of vegetables and fruits. The people and their possessions needed protection, and for many years special police were on guard. For a great many years he was captain of the Eleventh Ward Special Police, a body of men who risked many dangers at the hands of reckless characters, and who did service for many years without thought of monetary reward."[4]

NOTES

1. Plewe, Brandon S., et. at., *Mapping Mormonism* (Provo, Utah: Brigham Young University Press, 2012), 128.
2. *Chronicles of Courage,* Lesson Committee (Salt Lake City: Talon Printing, 1997), 8:105.
3. Dale F. Beecher, "The Office of Bishop." Dialogue 15 (Winter 1982): 103–15; Donald G. Pace, "Community Leadership on the Mormon Frontier: Mormon Bishops and the Political, Economic, and Social Development before Statehood." Ph.D. diss., Ohio State University, 1983).
4. Andrew Jenson, *L.D.S Biographical Encyclopedia* (Salt Lake City: Publishers Press, 1901) Vol. 1, 622.

Wine

Brigham Young stated in 1864, "I anticipate the day when we can have the privilege of using at our sacraments pure wine produced within our borders. I do not know that it would injure us to drink wine of our own make although we would be better without it than to drink it to excess."[1]

The sacramental consumption of wine was miniscule compared to what was produced. It was Brigham's goal to barrel the excess wine and sell it to the mining communities in Nevada and Southern Utah. Regardless of the Word of Wisdom, more wine was consumed in the

Church settlements than what the leaders cared to admit. In 1900 the Church put an end to producing and selling wine.[2]

NOTES

1. Leonard J. Arrington, An Economic Interpretation of the "Word of Wisdom," *BYU Studies,* Vol. 1, Issue 1, 1959, 46.
2. Ibid.

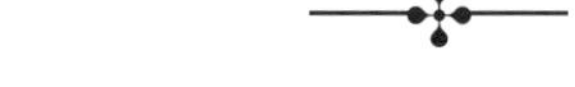

Word of Wisdom

Doctrine and Covenants 89 was received as an answer to an issue in the School of the Prophets. It was during January 1833 when Joseph Smith established the School of the Prophets. This school was organized to train elders in the church in doctrine and other secular topics. It appeared to be a ritual with the men attending to smoke their pipes and chew tobacco while listening to the Prophet instruct them. The task of cleaning the floor fell on the shoulders of Emma. The tobacco juice stained the floor, making the chore difficult. While inquiring of the Lord about the matter, Joseph received revelation in February 1833 known as the Word of Wisdom. In it the Lord instructs, "Tobacco is not for man but is for bruises & all sick cattle; to be used with judgement & skill."[1]

From the inception of this revelation, members were encouraged to obey its precepts. However, due to the habitual nature of tobacco and alcohol, not all members had the ability to rid their lives of these stimulants. This is the way it stood for decades, when at the turn of the century, discussion among those in the leading counsels of the Church continued the age old argument whether the Word of Wisdom was in fact a commandment. Some, like Lorenzo Snow, Joseph F. Smith, and Heber J. Grant believed all members should conform and follow the Lords law of health. Wilford Woodruff also believed it was a commandment of the Lord but felt that bishops should not withhold temple recommends from those who did not obey. Other leaders like Brigham Young Jr. and John Henry Smith believed that beer (or at least Danish beer) be exempt from the list of harmful stimulants. Some leaders consumed beer, wine, tea, and coffee. Believe it or not, there was a greater emphasis on the abstinence of red meat rather than alcohol and tobacco by some of the leaders.[2]

It wasn't until Joseph F. Smith became the prophet of the Church that the Word of Wisdom, the way we understand it, started to take shape. President Smith was fast to close down the bar at the Saltair resort on the shores of the Great Salt Lake. On July 5, 1906, the wine typically used during the sacrament in the temple meeting of the First Presidency and the Twelve was substituted with water. It wasn't until 1921 that adherence to the Word of Wisdom became a requirement for worthiness and temple participation.[3]

The following are some of the more anecdotal situations I've encountered in my readings through the years as it applies to the Word of Wisdom.

In 1859, Bishop Edward Hunter's counsel for the use of liquor by men in the Church was either leave it entirely alone or take it moderately. Brigham Young taught the harms of tobacco but realized that its use was common among Church members. His argument was, if you're going to use it, then why not raise it to cut down on the exorbitant cost of importation? Brigham Young pushed observance of the Word of Wisdom during the April 1867 general conference. He believed that the Word of Wisdom should be a matter of membership but backed off of this more stringent stance, realizing that some would think this severe. Instead, President Young counseled bishops to instruct their members to obey this commandment. The push was toward the younger generations, as it was believed that those who were older had used tobacco and alcohol to the point its use became habitual, realizing that this might snowball into other issues. Surprisingly, there was success, but only temporary success. It wasn't until the twentieth century when the Word of Wisdom finally became a matter of personal worthiness.[4]

Brigham Young shared the following from the pulpit in the old tabernacle in Salt Lake City in 1861:

> Many of the brethren chew tobacco and have advised them to be modest about it. Do not take out a whole plug of tobacco in

> meeting before the eyes of the congregation and cut off a long slice and put it in your mouth to the annoyance of everybody around. Do not glory in this disgraceful practice. If you must use tobacco put a small portion in your mouth when no person sees you and be careful that no one sees you chew it do not charge you with sin. You have the word of wisdom, read it some say oh as do in private so do in public and am not ashamed of it. It is at least disgraceful to expose your absurdities. Some men will go into a clean and beautifully furnished parlor with tobacco in their mouths and feel ask no odds. Would advise such men to be more modest and not spit upon the carpets and furniture but step to the door and be careful not to let any person see you spit or what is better omit chewing until you have an opportunity to do so without offending." Likewise at the fortieth annual conference of the saints in salt lake city in 1870 President Young similarly took time to chastise the members on Sunday after meeting "going through the gallery of the new tabernacle which had been occupied by those claiming no doubt to be gentlemen and perhaps brethren you might have supposed that cattle had been standing around there and dropping their nuisances here and there were great quids of tobacco and places a foot or two feet square smeared with tobacco juice. Wish the doorkeepers when in the future they observe any persons besmearing the seats and floor in this way to request them to leave the house and if they refuse and will not stop spitting about and besmearing their neighbors just take them and lead them out carefully and kindly. It is an imposition for those claiming to be gentlemen to spit tobacco juice for ladies to draw their clothes through and besmear them or to leave their dirt in the house. We request all addicted to this practice to omit it while in this house. Elders of Israel if you must chew tobacco omit it while in meeting and when you leave you can take a double portion if you wish to.[5]

It appears that it wasn't until the reorganization of the Relief Society in 1867, and the School of the Prophets, that there appeared to be a greater push to expect compliance from the Saints regarding the Word of Wisdom.[6] Also during this year, Brigham Young believed he might have more success speaking to the women of the church, rather than the men, when he asked them to abstain from the use of tea and coffee and urged them to train their families to do the same. He further stated:

You know that we all profess to believe the Word of Wisdom. There has been a great deal said about it more in former than in later years. We as latter day saints care but little about tobacco but as Mormons we use vast quantity of it. How much do you suppose goes annually from this territory and has for ten or twelve years past in gold and silver to supply the people with tobacco. I will say $60,000. Brother William H. Hooper our delegate in congress came here in 1849 and during about eight years he was selling goods. His sales for tobacco alone amounted to over $28,000 a year at the same time there were other stores that sold their share and drew their share of the money expended yearly besides what has been brought in by the keg and by the half keg. The traders and passing emigration have sold tons of tobacco besides what is sold here regularly. I say that $60,000 annually manually is the smallest figure. I can estimate the sales at tobacco can be raised here as well as it can be raised in any other place. It wants attention and care if we use it let us raise it here. I recommend for some man to go to raising tobacco. One man who came here last fall is going to do so and if he is diligent he will raise quite a quantity. I want to see some man go to and make a business of raising tobacco and stop sending money out of the territory for that article. Some of the brethren are very strenuous upon the Word of Wisdom and would like to have me preach upon it and urge it upon the brethren and make it a test of fellowship. I do not think that I shall do so I have never done so.[7]

NOTES

1. churchofjesuschrist.org/study/manual/revelations-in-context/the-word-of-wisdom?lang=eng
2. semanticscholar.org/paper/The-word-of-wisdom%3A-from-principle-to-requirement.-
3. semanticscholar.org/paper/The-word-of-wisdom%3A-from-principle-to-requirement.
4. Ronald W. Walker and Doris R. Dant ed., *Nearly Everything Imaginable (*Provo, Utah: BYU Press, 1999), 278.
5. Leonard J. Arrington, An Economic Interpretation of the "World of Wisdom," *BYU Studies,* Vol. 1, Issue 1, 1959, 41–42.
6. Ibid., 43.
7. Ibid., 45–46.

Young Women

In 1915 all young women, ages fourteen until they entered the Relief Society, were considered Beehives. Today, a young lady works on her Young Women Recognition award. However, back in those years the young women achieved advancement within the Beehives by completing various requirements. Believe it or not, there were 373 requirements that a Beehive could choose from to complete her award. The following is a sampling of twenty-three such requirements:

- Care successfully for a hive of bees for one season, and know their habits.
- Give the distinguishing characteristics of 6 varieties of hen and cattle and tell the good and weak points of each.
- Exterminate the mosquitoes over an area of ½ mile square by pouring a little kerosene on the surface of all standing pools of water twice each month during April, May, or June. Six girls may do this and each receive an award, or one girl can receive six awards.
- Make two articles of underwear by hand.
- Cover 25 miles on snowshoes in any six days.
- Learn to float in Great Salt Lake and propel yourself 50 feet.
- During three consecutive months, abstain from candy, ice cream, commercially manufactured beverages and chewing gum.
- For one month, masticate (chew) your food so thoroughly that it slips down without any visible effort at swallowing it.
- Successfully put a new washer on a faucet.
- Care for at least two kerosene lamps daily.
- For three months, take care of milk and cream from at least one cow and see that the pails, pans, strainer, and separator are thoroughly cleansed.
- During two weeks, keep the house free from flies or destroy at least 25 flies daily.
- Have your toilet [outhouse] moved to an isolated place in the garden. Have chicken wire built about three feet away and

plant quick-growing vines such as cucumber of morning glories to screen it from observation.

- Whitewash your toilet inside and out.
- Know and describe three cries of a baby.
- Without help or advice, care for and harness a team at least five times; driving fifty miles during one season.
- During 2 summer months, clean ice chest thoroughly twice a week.
- Discover ten reasons why the Columbine should be made the national flower.
- Clear sagebrush, etc. off of one-half acre of land.
- Know 6 blazes used by Indians.[1]

In 1950 the age group for the Beehives was changed to the age of twelve- and thirteen-year-old girls.

NOTE

1. churchofjesuschrist.org/training/womens-auxiliary-organizations/young-women-programs

About the Author

Dan Barker was raised in a family of accomplished artists. The family trait of creativity expressed itself in Dan's life by writing the stories of the pioneers, rather than through brush and paint. This passion for the early Saints was kindled by a family vacation along the famed Mormon Trail. Dan has returned on many occasions to the various Church history sites, and blessed to have been called to the New England States on his mission, where many of the pioneer stories began. Dan is the author of five books published by Cedar Fort. He and his wife reside in Pleasant Grove, Utah.

Notes

Notes

Notes